GANG WARS

GANG WARS

Blood and Guts on the Streets of Early New York

GANGSTER

by Hélèna Katz

PUBLISHED BY ALTITUDE PUBLISHING LTD.
1500 Railway Avenue, Canmore, Alberta T1W 1P6
www.altitudepublishing.com
1-800-957-6888

Extreme care has been taken to ensure that all information presented in
this book is accurate and up to date. Neither the author nor the
publisher can be held responsible for any errors.

Publisher	Stephen Hutchings
Associate Publisher	Kara Turner
Series Editor	Jill Foran
Digital Photo Colouring	Bryan Pezzi

We acknowledge the financial support of the Government
of Canada through the Book Publishing Industry Development
Program (BPIDP) for our publishing activities.

Altitude GreenTree Program
Altitude Publishing will plant twice as many trees as were used
in the manufacturing of this product.

Cataloging in Publication Data

Katz, Hélèna, 1964-
   Gang wars / Hélèna Katz.

(Amazing stories)
ISBN 1-55265-105-3

   1. Gangs--New York (State)--New York--History. I. Title. II. Series: Amazing
stories (Canmore, Alta.)

HV6439.U7N4 2005   364.1'06'6097471   C2005-902482-8

An application for the trademark for Amazing Stories™
has been made and the registered trademark is pending.

Printed and bound in Canada by Friesens
2 4 6 8 9 7 5 3 1

To my grandfather, Chaïm Pinchos Katz,
a journalist in prewar Poland with whom I share a
love for telling stories; and to my father, Selim Katz,
the thread that links me to a man I never knew.

Contents

Prologue

Owney Madden ordered his men to take all the furniture in the apartment and pile it up against the front door. A policeman had just come by to order the members of the Gopher Gang to pipe down, and Madden was certain he'd be back — and that he wouldn't come alone. The leader of the Gophers wanted his men to be ready. Once the furniture was sufficiently piled, Madden looked out the window. Sure enough, a phalanx of policemen was coming down the street.

Soon the voice of an officer could be heard on the other side of the door. The officer ordered Madden and his men to open up. They refused, and began to taunt the policeman instead. Undeterred, the officer banged his nightstick against the door, prompting one of the gang members to raise a gun and fire at him through the window. The glass shattered and the whole police squad fled. But not for long.

A little while later, the same officer walked up to the front door and initiated an argument with Madden and his buddy, Tanner Smith. As Madden threatened and derided the officer, other members of the Gophers crowded around to listen — their leader's tirade was just too entertaining to miss. Suddenly, the gang members felt the powerful sting of clubs hitting them. That's when they realized that a couple of the cops had somehow gotten inside the apartment. Moments later, the rest of the squad crashed through the front door. The Gophers had nowhere to go.

Chapter 1
On the Waterfront with the Daybreak Boys

I t was about 12:30 a.m. on August 25, 1852, when gangsters Nicholas Howlett, William Saul, and William Johnson left the saloon at 51 Cherry Street. The threesome tripped along the sidewalks of the Fourth Ward until they reached a rowboat at the foot of Dover Street. After greasing the oars (so they'd make less noise while rowing), Howlett and Saul climbed into the boat, laying a drunken Johnson along its bottom. The leaders of the Daybreak Boys were on the prowl for another vessel to plunder.

Howlett, Saul, and Johnson were among the estimated 500 river pirates in the area. Each of these pirates belonged to one of the 50 or so gangs that prowled the waterfront of the

East River under the cover of night, stealing everything they could from the docks and from visiting ships. These gangs were a product of the wretchedness of the Fourth Ward, which extended from south of New York's Bowery district to the waterfront. The Fourth Ward was such a dangerous place that even police officers were reluctant to patrol the area alone. For a good 25 years, Water Street, which was part of the ward and ran parallel to the East River, was the scene of more violent crime than any other street in North America. Almost every building along Water Street housed at least one saloon, dance hall, or brothel.

It hadn't always been this way. Before the American Revolution, and for almost 30 years afterwards, the Fourth Ward had been the finest residential neighborhood in New York. Cherry trees and handsome mansions had lined the streets, and upscale merchants had set up shop nearby. As the years passed, however, the young country lured more new settlers, and poor immigrants began pouring into the area. The neighborhood's aristocrats, in turn, began moving north.

By 1840, the lovely mansions had been replaced by rows of squalid apartment buildings that housed a poverty-stricken population. Among these buildings was Gotham Court, a double row of connected tenements that extended for 130 feet along Cherry Street and lodged more than 1000 people — most of them Irish. Along with being overcrowded, Gotham Court sat above one of the neighborhood's main sewers, and smells from underground would seep into the building. Even worse, rats the size of house cats would often come up through the pipes and bite at the residents. Local gangs, meanwhile, used the sewers to hide from police and stash the fruits of their thefts.

By 1845, the Fourth Ward was a hotbed of crime. The first river gang in the neighborhood to operate as an organized group was the Daybreak Boys. The members of this gang were known to be particularly brutal; most had committed at least one murder before the age of 20, and all had committed countless robberies. They were often aided in these endeavors by members of their junior gang — the Little Daybreak Boys. Members of the junior gang ranged from 8 to 12 years old and did everything they could to impress their namesakes. Not only would they act as lookouts or decoys during robberies, they would also risk their own necks on occasion by crawling through the portholes of targeted ships and lowering ropes so that the adults could climb aboard.

Nicholas Howlett and William Saul had "graduated" from the ranks of the junior gang when Saul was 16 years old and Howlett was 15. Together, the pair took over the helm of the Daybreak Boys in 1850 and quickly became the most illustrious leaders in the gang's history. Under Saul's and Howlett's leadership, the Daybreak Boys — who also included the likes of Slobbery Jim, Patsy the Barber, Sow Madden, and Cow-Legged Sam McCarthy — terrorized boat crews on the East River waterfront for the next two years. They also occasionally ventured into the more dangerous waters of the Hudson River and the harbor. Over the course of Saul's and Howlett's tenure as gang leaders, the Daybreak Boys stole more than $100,000 in property and committed at least 20 murders. The last of these known murders was committed in August 1852 ...

It was nearly 1 a.m. on August 25 when Saul and Howlett began to row as quietly as possible among the many ships docked between the piers, looking for one to rob. First they set their sights on a schooner, but as they neared their target they realized the watchman on board was still awake. So they rowed on, and soon settled on plundering a nearby brig. As Howlett scurried on board and walked towards the cabin door, a voice came from inside the cabin.

"Who is that?"

"It is I," Howlett responded, hoping to bluff his way inside.

"Who are you?" the voice demanded again. "What do you want?"

Realizing they were about to get caught, the leaders of the Daybreak Boys climbed back into their boat and paddled away. Moments later, they spotted a new target: the *Thomas Watson*, a two-masted sailing ship docked at the foot of Oliver Street.

After rowing up close to the ship, Howlett and Saul woke Johnson, who was still lying on the floor of the rowboat. It was obvious to both men that Johnson was far too drunk to be of any real use, so they left him there and told him to look after the boat. Then, quietly, without being noticed by anyone, they boarded the *Thomas Watson*.

The pair crept along the deck, careful not to make a sound. As they approached the cabin, they saw that the outer door was partly open. Peeking inside, they spotted the ship's night watchman, Charles Baxter, slumbering away on his back. The men grinned at each other. This would be a piece of cake.

It was decided that Saul would search the cabin while Howlett kept watch on deck. Before they parted ways, Howlett offered Saul his pistol. Saul took it and entered the cabin. He stepped over the sleeping Baxter and began to look around. After grabbing a pocket watch and a pair of pants, he quietly left the cabin and returned to Howlett. Handing his partner the pair of pants, Saul whispered that there was nothing more to steal.

Howlett wasn't convinced. He took off his shoes and went into the cabin, stepping over the snoring watchman. Saul was right behind him. Howlett opened the drawers of a bureau, but there was nothing interesting inside — only papers. As the twosome tried to open a door that led to another part of the boat, Baxter awoke. "Who's there?" he shouted, sitting up.

Realizing he needed to escape as quickly as possible, Howlett grabbed a stick from a table, took a swipe at the watchman, and darted out of the cabin. Saul followed shortly after, but not before aiming his gun and shooting the unarmed man in the neck. Charles Baxter fell to the floor instantly.

At the sound of the gunshot, first mate Robert Adams, who had also been asleep on the ship, woke with a start and quickly discovered the wounded Baxter lying on the cabin floor. Adams ran to the deck, hoping to catch whoever had shot his crewmate. But it was too late. The two Daybreak Boys had made it off the ship. Adams watched as they leapt into their small boat and pushed off from the dock. Then he began to yell for help.

Policeman Thomas Flanley had been standing on the corner of James and Cherry Streets when he heard the gunshot. He and another officer standing nearby quickly realized that the sound had come from the *Thomas Watson*. They rushed to the ship, and when Flanley reached the deck, he saw Baxter staggering up the stairs. "I am shot," Baxter told the police officer. While the other officer ran further up the dock, Flanley took care of the wounded watchman, carrying him to New York Hospital in a handcart.

Meanwhile, in their attempt to avoid the authorities, Saul and Howlett had boarded a nearby brig. Exhausted from their activities, they crawled into separate berths and fell asleep. As the twosome slumbered, word of the shooting spread among police officers in the area, and many of them began to search for the men who had wounded Baxter. In short order, Officer Charles Newton found the pair on the brig and arrested them. It was 3:30 a.m. when the two prisoners were brought, barefoot, to the Seventh Ward station house.

By this time, word had also reached the station house that the watchman on the *Thomas Watson* had been shot. The leaders of the Daybreak Boys were no strangers to the police, and it was clear to the officers that Howlett and Saul had been responsible for the shooting. An officer by the name of Nicholas Duffy identified a pair of patent leather shoes found on the *Thomas Watson* as belonging to Howlett — the Daybreak Boy had been wearing the same shoes a week earlier when Duffy had arrested him for disorderly conduct.

Baxter, a father of four children, died at 4 a.m. on August 25 — only two days after joining the crew of the *Thomas Watson*. By noon, a coroner had empaneled a jury and taken them to New York Hospital to see Baxter's body. Saul and Howlett were brought to the City Prison (more commonly referred to as "the Tombs") while the coroner continued his investigation. William Johnson was also found and arrested. The three men laughed when they were told they'd be tried for Baxter's murder. Somehow, they were certain they would never be convicted. To their shock, all three were found guilty of murder. Johnson was sentenced to life in prison, while Saul and Howlett were condemned to death. The governor refused appeals for clemency.

On the morning of January 28, 1853, the two leaders of the Daybreak Boys were brought from their cells to the courtyard of the Tombs. They were placed on the scaffold before a crowd of more than 200 spectators. Many people in the crowd walked past the scaffold, stopping to shake hands with the two condemned men. Once the crowd had settled, William Saul, age 21, and Nicholas Howlett, age 20, were put to death.

This would prove to be the beginning of the end for the Daybreak Boys. Shortly after Saul and Howlett were hanged, gang members Slobbery Jim and Bill Lowrie took over as leaders. However, Slobbery Jim's high rank as leader was short-lived. Within months of gaining this position, he was prowling the waterfront with fellow gang member Patsy the Barber. As they wandered along the docks, they spotted a German immigrant who hadn't been in New York City for long. The pair snuck up behind the man and hit him with a club. Once he was unconscious, they robbed him of all his money, which amounted to 12 cents, and pushed his body into the harbor, where he drowned. Now 12 cents richer, the twosome headed to the Hole-in-the-Wall Saloon on Water Street to divide up the money.

A man named One-Armed Charley Monell ran the Hole-in-the-Wall Saloon, with the help of a six-foot-tall Englishwoman known as Gallus Mag. She had earned her nickname because she wore suspenders, or galluses, to keep her skirt up. Gallus Mag was the bouncer at the Hole-in-the-Wall and she ruled over the place with a pistol in her belt and a huge bludgeon strapped to her wrist. People were afraid of her — and with good reason. Even the police of the era thought she was the most savage woman they had ever known. She had a habit of using her club to calm difficult customers. Then, once a rowdy customer was pacified, she would clutch his ear between her teeth and drag him towards the door as onlookers cheered. If the customer tried to fight back, she would bite off his ear and toss him into the street. Each piece of ear that Gallus Mag bit was considered a trophy, and she would march behind the bar and put the newest piece into a jar of alcohol to be pickled.

When Slobbery Jim and Patsy the Barber arrived at the Hole-in-the-Wall, they quickly got down to business. Slobbery Jim figured he should get 7 and maybe even 8 of the 12 cents, since he was the one who had hoisted the heavy German into the harbor. But Patsy the Barber thought they should divide the money equally because he was the one who had clubbed the German into unconsciousness. He pointed out that if he hadn't done that, Slobbery Jim wouldn't have been able to push their victim into the water in the first place.

Livid, Slobbery Jim grabbed Patsy the Barber's big nose between his teeth. Patsy retaliated by pulling out a knife and shoving it between Jim's ribs. This, however, did little damage, and the two men began to wrestle on the floor of the saloon. One-Armed Charley and Gallus Mag didn't intervene; they assumed the two Daybreak Boys were fighting for a good reason.

Slobbery Jim finally managed to grab the knife from Patsy the Barber and, in short order, he stabbed Patsy in the throat. The wounded man fainted from the immediate loss of blood. Slobbery Jim then finished him off by stomping him to death with his hobnailed boots. When his job was done, he fled the Hole-in-the-Wall and was never seen again.

Not long after Slobbery Jim's disappearance, another Daybreak leader ran into some bad luck — Bill Lowrie was arrested for a robbery on the docks and sent to prison for 15 years. Cow-Legged Sam McCarthy took over what remained of the Daybreak Boys, but abandoned the floundering gang soon after, defecting to a gang in the Five Points that committed burglaries in residential and manufacturing areas further uptown.

With the loss of five leaders in a matter of months, the Daybreak Boys had been dealt a heavy blow. The last nail was pounded into the gang's coffin when local authorities finally agreed to set up a harbor police patrol that would protect the docks. The police had been lobbying for such a patrol for years, certain it was the only way to stamp out the river pirates.

The harbor police began patrolling on March 15, 1858. At first, only a few officers toured the rivers and lower harbor in rowboats, examining any suspicious-looking craft. Within a few days, however, other policemen joined the fold. They concentrated their efforts on the Daybreak Boys, who were already demoralized by their loss of various leaders and the defection of key members.

By 1859, the Daybreak Boys were completely wiped out.

But the group had nevertheless left its mark on the area's history. As the first — and certainly most notorious — of the Fourth Ward's organized river gangs, the Daybreak Boys and their antics became known far and wide. Their demise and the addition of a harbor police patrol ensured that ships and their crews would finally be able to carry out their work more safely.

Chapter 2
The Dead Rabbits and the Bowery Boys

Tension was mounting and dissension among the ranks growing as members of the Roach Guards continued to argue. Suddenly, in the midst of the squabbling, someone hurled the carcass of a dead rabbit into the middle of the room. Stunned at the odd turn of events, one of the fighting factions decided it was time to leave the gang for good. Soon after, members of this group formed their own gang and called themselves the Dead Rabbits. From then on, they carried a dead rabbit, impaled on a pike, whenever they went into battle.

The Dead Rabbits and the Roach Guards were among the many gangs that flourished in New York's Five Points district in the first half of the 19th century. Other gangs in the neighborhood at that time included the Chichesters, the Plug Uglies, and the Shirt Tails. All were brutal, and all spent much of their time roaming the district looking for fights.

The Five Points was one of the toughest areas in the United States. It earned its name because it sat at the intersection of five streets: Little Water, Cross, Anthony, Orange, and Mulberry. In the center of the neighborhood sat a small open space called Paradise Square.

The streets around Paradise Square were lined with dance halls, tenements, and saloons. During the 1820s, immigrants, mostly "low-class Irish," moved into the area. Shortly after, small greengroceries started springing up around the Five Points. While these stores featured racks of vegetables on display out front, their backrooms offered a different sort of product: cheap alcohol. As a result, gangs of thugs, pickpockets, thieves, and murderers would congregate in these backrooms on a regular basis.

Meanwhile, the nearby Bowery district had plenty of dives of its own. The Bowery, which began at Chatham Square and extended for a mile to Cooper Square, was home to more native-born residents than the Five Points. However, like the Five Points, it had its own group of gangs, including the Atlantic Guards, the American Guards, the True Blue Americans, and the Bowery Boys. These gangs, like those in the Five Points, often warred amongst one another. On certain occasions, though, they put aside their differences to unite against one or several of the Five Points gangs. Indeed, the enmity between gangs in the same district was nothing compared to the tension between gangs from neighboring regions.

The rivalry between the Bowery Boys and the Dead Rabbits was particularly fierce. Most of the Bowery Boys were more prosperous than their counterparts in the Five Points. They held jobs as butchers, mechanic's apprentices, or bouncers in one of the Bowery saloons or dance halls. They were part of the working poor, while the Dead Rabbits were part of the underclass. Each gang strongly resented the other.

For many years, the Bowery Boys and the Dead Rabbits waged frequent battles throughout the Sixth Ward, which encompassed both of their neighborhoods. These battles often lasted for several days. Gang members on both sides would crowd behind barricades constructed of piled carts and paving stones and use whatever weapons they could. Sometimes they fired at each other with muskets and pistols. Other times they got closer to their opponents and used knives, brickbats, bludgeons, teeth, and fists. When a man fell in battle, his enemies showed him no mercy. They jumped on him, kicking and stamping him to death. On more than one occasion, the city had to call in the National Guard or the regular army to try to separate the two sides.

Though armed services were able to stop the fighting on a few isolated occasions, the day-to-day conditions in New York's Lower East Side remained ideal for illegal activity. It wasn't hard for gang members to roam the streets unchecked because there weren't enough policemen to enforce the law. Moreover, the few policemen who *were* around weren't properly trained. Inefficient policing also made it easier for local politicians to join forces with the local gangs.

In the 1820s, Tammany Hall, a Democratic organization, realized that the most effective way to manipulate people's votes was to create an alliance between politicians and gang members. Gangs like the Dead Rabbits could intimidate a political leader's opponents at the polls and provide people who would vote more than once on election day. While these tactics helped Tammany Hall gain power and control municipal politics, they also benefited the gangs, whose other illegal activities were suddenly protected by elected officials.

The ties between gangs and politicians grew stronger with the arrival of two very powerful men — Isaiah Rynders and John Morrissey. Rynders was a former Mississippi River gambler and bowie knife fighter who came to New York in the mid-1830s. Soon after he arrived, he bought half a dozen greengroceries and a saloon. Through these acquisitions he managed to secure control of the Five Points and used the district's gangs to rule the affairs of the Sixth Ward. Rynders quickly gained influence in Tammany Hall politics.

Then, sometime in the late 1840s, Irish-born John Morrissey arrived in New York and began hanging around Rynders' saloon. Boasting a string of criminal indictments and a brutally violent streak, Morrissey claimed he could beat up anyone in the joint. Although one taker beat him soundly, Morrissey nonetheless managed to impress Rynders, who promptly hired him as an enforcer. In this role, Morrissey imposed the political will of his boss with threats and violence.

During a local election in 1850, Morrissey was hired by Tammany politician John A. Kennedy to once again control voting at the polls. Morrissey's main challenge in this endeavor would be outsmarting his archrival, Bill "the Butcher" Poole. A member of the Bowery Boys before heading his own gang, the American-born Poole was against Tammany politics. In an effort to keep Kennedy out of office, Poole vowed that his men would attack the polling place in the Sixth Ward and destroy the ballot boxes. In response to this threat, Morrissey recruited 50 members of the Dead Rabbits and paid each of them a dollar to protect the polling place. He stationed them throughout the building and ordered them to beat up Poole's men when they arrived.

The Dead Rabbits didn't have to wait long for their rivals to appear. Poole arrived at around noon with 30 thugs in tow. They swarmed the building, but stopped dead in their tracks when they saw the Dead Rabbits waiting for them. Poole and Morrissey came face to face in the middle of the polling station, staring each other down. Finally, realizing he was terribly outnumbered, Poole stalked out of the building with his men behind him — but it wouldn't be the last time that Morrissey and Poole faced off against each other.

The feud between the two men intensified in the

early 1850s because of the growing popularity of a political movement that favored native-born Americans and sought to curtail the political power of Irish and other immigrants. Poole championed the Nativist movement and became a leader in the Native American, or Know-Nothing, Party. The Nativist movement called for liquor restrictions and opposed the election of foreign-born Americans to political office. The Democrats of Tammany Hall, meanwhile, opposed the laws that would restrict the sale of alcohol. They also favored immigrants.

In 1854, Poole beat Morrissey in a boxing match on the Christopher Street pier. The two rivals then agreed to meet for a rematch on the Amos Street dock at seven o'clock the next morning. When Morrissey arrived at the dock with a dozen of his supporters, Poole was nowhere to be found — but 200 of his bruisers were present. Some of these thugs started to beat up Morrissey and continued to do so until a group of Tammany toughs heard what was happening and came to rescue him.

Morrissey and Poole crossed paths again on February 24, 1855. That night, Poole stopped in for a pint of champagne at Stanwix Hall, a nice new saloon on Broadway. Morrissey was already inside playing cards when he heard Poole's voice. Poole was boasting about his exceptional fighting skills. Unwilling to let these boasts go unchallenged, Morrissey approached Poole, drew his gun, and pulled the trigger. Alas, the gun didn't fire. Poole then drew his own gun, but put it away when someone said, "You wouldn't shoot an unarmed man, would you?"

Instead, Poole challenged Morrissey to a duel with knives. Morrissey declined — Poole was, after all, a butcher, and certainly knew how to wield a knife. The police arrived just at that moment and arrested them both. They were subsequently released on the condition that they both go home and stay there. Morrissey followed the order, but Poole decided to return to the Stanwix for more drinking and boasting. Morrissey's friends — California Jim Turner, Lew Baker, and Paudeen McLaughlin — were still in the bar, and none of them was pleased to see Poole. They figured the time had come to put an end to the bragging once and for all. Turner shot Poole in the leg, and Baker shot him in the chest and abdomen. Before he crumpled to the floor, Poole managed to throw a knife in the direction of his attackers, but it missed them completely and lodged in the doorjamb. Two weeks later, Poole died of his injuries. He was a month shy of his 32nd birthday.

His followers considered him a martyr. At his funeral, Poole's body was preceded by a 52-piece band and followed by a procession of 2000 men. Some 600 members of the Know-Nothing Party followed his coffin, which was draped with the American flag. His body was taken down Broadway in an open hearse pulled by four white horses. An estimated 100,000 people from New York and surrounding areas came to pay their respects and watch as thugs and respectable men marched together in the funeral procession.

Bill "the Butcher" Poole's violent end only served to deepen the political rivalry between the Democrats and the Nativists. About two months prior to Poole's death, Fernando Wood had become the mayor of New York City after being elected by a narrow margin. Born in Philadelphia on June 14, 1812, Wood had settled in New York with his family in 1821. Before entering politics, he had run a grocery and liquor store at the corner of Washington and Recter Streets, one block from the busy waterfront. His business was very profitable, and as his earnings increased, so did his power. Wood soon became a member of Tammany Hall, where he used the Five Points gangs under Rynders to win the 1854 mayoral election.

Wood's re-election two years later was marred by unprecedented violence and voter fraud. The owners of the city's gambling houses and saloons, including Isaiah Rynders and John Morrissey, firmly supported Wood. The Dead Rabbits backed Wood, too, while the Bowery Boys backed the pro-Nativist candidate, Isaac O. Barker. The Nativists accused Wood of giving preferential treatment to the Irish and other foreigners. Reformers also opposed the corrupt mayor, who was using the city's coffers to dole out favors to his friends and allies.

At that time, an estimated 30,000 men in New York were loyal to gang leaders — and in turn to Tammany Hall or the Native American Party. During each civic election, thugs hired by rival parties would riot at polling places, smash ballot boxes, and slug honest citizens who tried to vote. In order to secure his re-election, Wood decided to take great advantage of these gang activities. He sent most of the police force off duty the night before the election, giving them strict instructions not to go near the polling places unless they were casting a ballot.

Not surprisingly, large-scale rioting broke out on election day, particularly in the heart of the Sixth Ward, where the Dead Rabbits and the Bowery Boys faced off in yet another battle. Initially, the Dead Rabbits scattered when the Bowery Boys arrived at the Sixth Ward polling place and caught their rivals by surprise. However, after regrouping and recruiting reinforcements from saloons and tenements in Paradise Square, the Dead Rabbits returned to the scene, armed with clubs, knives, axes, brickbats, and pistols. They showed no mercy as they attacked their enemies.

As the Dead Rabbits and Bowery Boys duked it out, chaos reigned in other wards, too. Gangs in the Fourth Ward destroyed ballot boxes, and in the First Ward, a voter's nose was shot off. In the end, Wood beat his political opponent, despite allegations that 10,000 fraudulent votes had been cast. He began his second term as mayor of New York City on January 1, 1857.

On April 15, 1857, the New York State legislature passed a bill to create a metropolitan police district that included New York, Kings, Westchester, and Richmond Counties. Rather than being managed by the mayor, this police force would be controlled by a five-member board of commission-ers appointed by the governor with the consent of the sen-ate. The local police forces of New York and Brooklyn would be disbanded.

Mayor Wood did not want to relinquish his control over policing in the city. With the support of his aldermen, Wood ignored the legislative act and refused to surrender police property or power. As a result, New York City soon had two police departments — a municipal one under Wood's con-trol, and a metropolitan one under state control. The situa-tion was a disaster for honest citizens, but ideal for criminals. Whenever an officer from the metropolitan department arrested someone, a municipal policeman would arrive on the scene and challenge the other officer's jurisdiction. While the two peace officers argued and swiped at each other with their clubs, the criminal would walk away.

The Dead Rabbits and Bowery Boys took advantage of this chaos to perpetuate their longstanding rivalry, brawling at every opportunity. The violence in the Sixth Ward escalated to new heights when word spread around the Five Points that Wood was finally going to disband the municipal police force. On July 2, the New York State Court of Appeals had declared the new police act constitutional. People in the Five Points believed the police act would disenfranchise foreign-born citizens by not allowing them to be members of the force. Their concerns were well founded: the Metropolitan Police Board hadn't appointed any Irishmen to the new force, save for the occasional Irish Republican.

Just after midnight on July 4, a metropolitan policeman was trying to make an arrest on the corner of Mulberry and Chatham Streets. Suddenly, a mob of gangsters from the Five Points surrounded him, beating him so severely that he later died of his injuries. About an hour after the beating, a crowd of nearly 100 Five Pointers, mostly members of the Dead Rabbits and Plug Uglies, congregated at Chatham Street, planning to beat up every new policeman they could find. Heading towards the Bowery, they stumbled upon a metropolitan officer just north of Bayard Street. They managed to wrestle his club from him before he fled down the street and ducked into a saloon that was known as the headquarters of the Bowery Boys. The people inside the saloon barricaded themselves as the Five Points gang members pelted the building with rocks and bricks. In no time, however, the rioters were distracted by the sight of another police officer slipping away from the scene. They chased him into a second saloon, but a large group of Bowery Boys arrived about 10 minutes later. Catching the Dead Rabbits and Plug Uglies by surprise, the Bowery Boys forced their enemies back into the Five Points.

As they retreated towards Paradise Square, members of the Dead Rabbits viciously attacked a group of men who just happened to be out in the street, fatally wounding one of them. Then, as dawn broke over the Sixth Ward, a number of gang members from both the Five Points and the Bowery claimed positions on the roofs of houses and tenements. From their new vantage points, these rioters were able to shoot pistols and muskets and shower brickbats on their enemies in the streets below. The fighting grew worse as the day progressed, and stretcher-bearers could be seen weaving in and out of buildings and alleyways, carrying away the wounded.

Later in the day, about two dozen Sixth Ward patrolmen left their barracks and were attacked on Bayard Street by a group of Dead Rabbits, who showered them with stones, bricks, fragments of ironware, and even some pots and kettles from the windows and rooftops of nearby tenements. A few minutes later, more than 100 Bowery Boys arrived and joined in the fray. The Dead Rabbits managed to repel their opponents, who backed up along Bayard Street until they reached a construction site. The bricks at the site proved to be handy weapons for tossing at the Dead Rabbits, who quickly retreated.

In the early hours of July 5, the Roach Guards joined the Dead Rabbits and the Plug Uglies, jumping readily into the skirmish. Together, the three Five Points gangs attacked a saloon near the Bowery. Called the Green Dragon, it was a popular hangout for the Bowery Boys. The Five Pointers swarmed the building, tearing it apart with iron bars and paving stones. They wrecked the ballroom, ripped the floor of the dance hall, and drank the supply of liquor. When news reached the Bowery Boys that one of their favorite hangouts was under attack, they rushed to the scene, along with their fellow Bowery gang, the Atlantic Guards. The Five Pointers, who had already left the Green Dragon, were intercepted by their enemies near the corner of Bayard and Chatham Streets. Inevitably, another battle broke out.

During the fighting, a metropolitan policeman made the mistake of trying to intervene. He clubbed his way through the crowd in a vain attempt to reach and arrest the ringleaders. He was knocked down, beaten up, stripped, and sent back to the White Street headquarters in his underwear. When he arrived at the precinct, panting and gasping, he told his colleagues about the riot. In short order, a detachment of metropolitan officers was marching to the scene, out for revenge.

As much as the gangs disliked one another, they hated the police even more. Suddenly, the archrivals from the Five Points and the Bowery teamed up to attack the metropolitan officers. After a bloody combat, the police somehow got the mob to retreat. But the rioting wasn't over. Many of the gang members once again fled to the upper stories and roofs of nearby buildings and rained bricks and stones on the police below. The police fled, having arrested only two people.

The riot grew in size as reinforcements for everyone — the Bowery gangs, the Five Points gangs, and the police — arrived from all over the city. At the height of the conflict, an estimated thousand rioters were involved in the bloody melee. The mayhem also attracted thieves and looters who were not linked to the gangs. Knowing the police would be busy with the rioters, these independents hit shops and homes throughout the Sixth Ward. Storeowners and saloon-keepers barricaded their buildings and tried to protect their property with muskets and pistols.

Whenever there was a lull in the fighting, women from the Five Points would scream taunts at their men, accusing them of being cowards. Spurred on by the stinging words, the Dead Rabbits and the rest of the Five Pointers would launch yet another attack. Many of the men who fell wounded on the sidewalks or streets were trampled.

Not knowing what else to do, the police commissioner, Simeon Draper, sent more policemen in to try to stop the rioters. These men marched in close formation towards the riot, coming up behind the Dead Rabbits and clearing the street as they went. They chased a number of Dead Rabbits and Bowery Boys into nearby houses and onto the roofs, hitting them with clubs as they went. One gangster who refused to give himself up was knocked off the roof of a house on Baxter Street. His skull was fractured when he hit the sidewalk, and his enemies stomped him to death.

The police managed to arrest about a dozen people before fleeing to White Street to avoid the growing crowd. After their departure, the warring gangs once again focused on each other. The Dead Rabbits forced the Bowery Boys to retreat to Elizabeth Street, where the Bowery Boys made another barricade out of carts, wagons, and construction materials. The Dead Rabbits followed suit. The gangsters then began to launch bricks at each other from behind their shelters.

By 6 p.m., the rioters were firing guns from behind the barricades. The number of dead and injured mounted as the two gangs continued fighting. One seemingly fearless member of the Dead Rabbits stood on top of a brick pile for about 15 minutes, heaving bricks at the Bowery Boys while dodging the bullets that whizzed around him.

Another member of the Dead Rabbits showed no fear as he walked calmly back and forth in front of his barricade. His opponents kept firing at him, but he was such a good shot that he killed two Bowery Boys with his pistol and wounded two others. As this was happening, a young boy whose brother was fighting with the Bowery Boys squirmed on his belly towards the enemy. Once he got close enough, he heaved a heavy brickbat at the Dead Rabbit's head. His aim was true, and the thug collapsed and lost consciousness.

The police kept trying to disperse the gangs but were continuously forced to retreat. Isaiah Rynders, who had been rewarded for his party loyalty by being made a United States marshal, arrived on the scene at 7 p.m. Standing in front of the barricades, he pleaded for an end to the fighting. Members of both sides jeered at him — even his own men were refusing to obey. Flustered beyond measure, Rynders went to the office of Police Commissioner Draper and demanded that the military be called in to stop the rioters. Nothing else, it seemed, could stop them. The commissioner asked Major General Charles Sandford to send over reinforcements.

At 9 p.m. that night, the sounds of bugles and drums could be heard as two regiments advanced towards the rioting gangs. They walked down White and Worth Streets, their numbers strengthened by two detachments of 75 policemen each. As they made their way through the battling horde, the police officers walked ahead of the army, clearing a path by clubbing the rioters. This display of force by the police and the National Guard was enough to stop the exhausted rioters, who realized they were outnumbered and overpowered. Suddenly, gang members who had been fighting for two days straight were fleeing in all directions. Although the riot was over, the military stayed in the streets all night.

The next day, residents of the Five Points began to search for missing loved ones, wanting to know whether they were dead or alive, safe or injured. Officially, there were 8 dead and more than 100 wounded, but it was widely rumored that gang members on both sides had taken away their own dead and secretly buried them in alleys and tunnels.

The riots on the streets of the Lower East Side that July were among the bloodiest in New York City's history.

Chapter 3

The Five Pointers and the Eastman Gang Duke it Out

When gang leader Monk Eastman walked down the streets of New York, he usually had a cat tucked under one arm and several others trailing behind him. What's more, a great blue pigeon that he'd tamed often sat perched on his shoulder. "I like de kits and boids," Eastman used to say. "I'll beat up any guy dat gets gay wit' a kit or a boid in my neck of de woods." It was said that Eastman owned 500 pigeons and more than 100 cats.

With the exception of the pets that followed him wherever he went, the leader of the Eastman Gang looked every bit a gangster. He had a bullet-shaped head, a short neck, a crooked nose, and numerous knife scars that gave him a ferocious air. He usually wore a derby hat that was much too small for his head, and he had bristly, unruly hair.

Monk Eastman was born in the Williamsburg section of Brooklyn in 1873. The son of a respectable Jewish restaurateur, his real name was Edward Osterman. When Eastman showed a love for cats and pigeons at an early age, his father set him up in his own pet shop. Eastman was barely 20 years old at the time, and being a storekeeper was too tame an activity for the young man. He grew restless and abandoned the pet shop in the mid-1890s to become a bouncer at the New Irving Dance Hall in Manhattan.

Eastman was ideal bouncer material. Not only was he skilled at wielding the huge club he carried, he was also an expert at using the blackjack he kept in his hip pocket and the brass knuckles that adorned each of his hands. Though he stood only 5 feet, 5 inches tall and weighed in at 150 pounds, he was a capable boxer and a strong fighter who knew what to do with a beer bottle or a piece of pipe in a pinch.

Indeed, the kindness that Eastman showed to cats and birds didn't extend to humans. Within a year of becoming a bouncer, he had cracked scores of heads. He bragged that during his first six months at the New Irving Dance Hall, 50 of the men he had beaten up had required hospitalization. His penchant for violence led ambulance drivers at the Bellevue Hospital to nickname the accident and emergency ward the "Eastman Ward."

After leaving his job at the New Irving Dance Hall,

Eastman struck out on his own as a gang leader. Having developed quite a following during his time as a bouncer, he had no trouble recruiting members — young men who admired and imitated Eastman joined his gang by the hundreds. Meanwhile, boys who were too young to join the main gang joined the Monk Eastman Juniors. By this time, the numerous small gangs that had roamed the Five Points and the Bowery in the mid-1800s had all but disappeared, replaced by larger groups with much more power.

The Eastman Gang was made up of about 1200 members, and it dominated the stretch of New York from the Bowery to the East River, and from Monroe to 14th Street. The gang's headquarters were located at an unsavory bar on Chrystie Street, near the Bowery, where Eastman could often be found lounging around inside without a shirt.

The main rival of the Eastman Gang was the Five Points Gang, a powerful group that had risen from the ashes of the Dead Rabbits, the Plug Uglies, and the Whyos of the Five Points district. The Five Pointers ruled an area between Broadway and the Bowery, and 14th Street and City Hall Park. Their headquarters were located at the New Brighton Dance Hall, which was owned by the gang's leader, Paul Kelly.

If Eastman looked every bit the gangster, Paul Kelly looked the opposite. Born Paolo Vaccarelli, the head of the Five Points Gang was small, soft-spoken, and usually neatly dressed in suits. Although he'd once been a professional bantamweight prizefighter, he seldom participated in brawls.

Kelly was a self-educated and cultured man who was fluent in English, French, Spanish, and Italian. An effective organizer, he had close to 1500 gang members under his command.

Both Eastman and Kelly had close ties to Tammany Hall politicians, and both leaders supplied repeaters (men who used fake names to vote several times) at the polls during elections. These repeaters also used violence to prevent honest citizens from trying to cast their ballots. And, if they were arrested for their efforts, they could rely on Tammany lawyers and bail bondsmen to get them out of trouble. Other gang activities at that time included pickpocketing operations, loft burglaries, and, occasionally, maiming or murder for hire. Members of both gangs had interests in brothels as well as in card games, which flourished on the East Side.

Although the Eastman Gang and the Five Pointers each had their own territory, they had an ongoing feud over an area between the Bowery and the Pelham Club on Pell Street. Monk Eastman claimed that the Five Pointers' territory ended at the Pelham, while Paul Kelly insisted it ended beyond the Pelham, at the Bowery, and that he was therefore entitled to whatever benefits he could scare up in the Bowery. Seldom did a week go by without thugs from both sides entering this no man's land armed with blackjacks and revolvers. They had orders to injure or kill every opposing gangster they found within the disputed territory.

The skirmishes and turf disputes between the two gangs continued to escalate. In April 1901, Eastman was out wandering alone in the Bowery when four members of the Five Points Gang attacked him near Chatham Square. The Five Pointers were armed with blackjacks and revolvers, while the only weapons Eastman had were his brass knuckles and slung shot. Nevertheless, Eastman fought back and managed to knock down three of his attackers. The fourth attacker, however, evaded the gang leader and then shot him twice in the stomach. Eastman crumpled to the ground and the four men fled, leaving Eastman for dead on the sidewalk. Somehow, he managed to get to his feet. Placing his fingers over his gaping wound, he staggered to Gouverneur Hospital.

The leader of the Eastman Gang was at death's door for several weeks, but he refused to give police the name of his shooter. Instead, he told detectives he would take care of the matter himself. As he lay recovering in his hospital bed, he worked out a revenge plan in his head. Just a week after Eastman was released from the hospital, his shooter was found dead in the gutter at the intersection of Grand and Chrystie Streets. Eastman had taken care of the matter with an underworld settling of accounts. But the feud between the two gangs continued for the next two years.

The warfare between the Eastman Gang and the Five Pointers affected areas beyond the gangs' turf. Sometimes their bullets strayed, hitting bystanders and smashing windows. As the animosity intensified, gangsters would scurry through the darkened streets of the East Side, shooting at each other from carriages or cars. Others would hide in doorways and pounce on their enemies without warning. Gangsters also interrupted balls and other social functions in the New Irving and Walhalla Halls to shoot at each other, never worrying about the innocent patrons who might be caught in the crossfire. Sometimes police officers would arrive in time to break up a fight, using their clubs to hit men on both sides of the dispute. Though arrests were often made, the gangs' strong political connections with Tammany Hall meant that protection was available whenever members of either gang were in trouble with the law.

The skirmishes between the two gangs came to a head on a hot summer night in August 1903. That evening, a card game was taking place under the Allen Street arch of the Second Avenue elevated railroad, which was in Eastman territory. As was the custom, once the game was over, its owner would faithfully give a percentage of the take to Monk Eastman.

At about 11 p.m., a group of Five Pointers arrived to raid the game and escape with the take. Six members of the Eastman Gang, however, had spotted the Five Pointers as they were making their way to the arch and figured their rivals were up to no good. Aware that a card game was taking place, the Eastmans quickly deduced what the Five Pointers had in mind. They followed their rivals to the arch and opened fire, instantly killing one of them. His buddies fired back, and the gang members exchanged several more shots before running for cover behind the pillars of the elevated railroad structure. For the next half-hour, members of both gangs took turns coming out from behind the pillars to shoot at the enemy. Two policemen arrived on the scene to try to stop the gunfight but ended up fleeing down Rivington Street in a hail of bullets — they would require some backup.

The police weren't the only ones who needed reinforcements. Each gang sent a messenger to its respective headquarters to let the other members know what was going on. A short time later, men began to arrive to bolster the numbers on both sides. Eastman gathered a group of his men at the Chrystie Street saloon and led them down to the gunfight. Placing himself behind an elevated pillar for protection, he directed his men at the scene of the battle. By midnight, more than 100 gunmen from each side had arrived. The two gangs were evenly matched in numbers as they blazed away at each other.

In the midst of the gun battle, half a dozen members of a third gang wandered into the fray. These young men were part of the Gophers, a large group based in Hell's Kitchen. Always looking for action, the Gophers found the opportunity to participate in the fighting too tempting to ignore. Without bothering to find out why the Eastmans and Five Pointers were fighting, they joyfully jumped into battle, shooting indiscriminately at both gangs. As one member of the Gophers later put it, "A lot of guys was poppin' at each other, so why shouldn't we do a little poppin' ourselves?"

With all the shooting that was taking place, innocent

people in the area were worried about stray bullets coming their way. The neighborhood's storekeepers barricaded their doors and windows, while residents of the local tenements locked themselves in their rooms. When officers from several police stations finally arrived to break up the gunfight, the mayhem had hit fever pitch. By the time the gangs were subdued, 3 people were dead, 7 were wounded, and another 20 were arrested.

Monk Eastman was among those detained. He told police his name was Joseph Morris — one of his many aliases. When questioned about his involvement in the gun battle, Eastman claimed that he'd just happened to be wandering by when he'd heard the shooting and, like any good rubbernecker, he'd simply stopped to see what was going on. He was arraigned the following morning and a magistrate immediately released him.

The shootout had generated a lot of media attention and the bosses at Tammany Hall were unhappy. While the politicians didn't mind an occasional shooting, murder, or blackjacking in the name of business, they felt the gangs were out of control. The war between the Eastman Gang and the Five Pointers was costing the lives of civilians. The Wild West shootouts had to stop.

A few days after the incident, Tammany district leader Tom Foley brought Paul Kelly and Monk Eastman together at the Palm Cafe on Chrystie Street in an effort to mediate a settlement between the two gangs. Eastman and Kelly fully understood the implication of the compulsory meeting: Tammany Hall would no longer protect the gangs' interests if the gunfights didn't stop.

The two leaders agreed to put an end to the hostilities. As part of the agreement, a strip of turf between the Pelham Club and the Bowery sidewalk a block away was declared neutral territory. Pleased with the outcome of the meeting, Foley held a ball to celebrate the peace treaty. In the midst of the celebrations, Kelly and Eastman met at the center of the dance floor and ceremoniously shook hands. Then the members of the Five Pointers and the Eastmans danced the night away.

The truce, however, was short-lived. It ended several months later when a member of the Eastman Gang and a member of the Five Pointers began to argue over whose leader was braver. The argument turned ugly and the two men began fighting. The Five Pointer broke his opponent's nose in two places and twisted one of his ears off.

Monk Eastman was outraged when he found out. He immediately sent a message to Paul Kelly, warning him that if he didn't handle the matter and get the perpetrator out of the way, the Eastmans would invade the Five Pointers' turf and get revenge. Kelly then sent a message of his own to Eastman: the Eastman Gang was welcome to the Five Pointer in ques- tion — if they could catch him.

The rivalry between the two gangs heated up all over again. Tammany politicians organized another meeting with

Kelly and Eastman. This time, neutral observers were present. The two gang leaders arrived at the Palm Cafe with armed bodyguards. They shook hands with great formality and then sat down to negotiate how to retain their honor while keeping their thugs from attacking each other.

Since the prowess of the two gang leaders had been at the heart of the brawl between their underlings, Eastman and Kelly agreed to face each other in a boxing match that would decide which of them was supreme. They set a time and place, and also agreed on how many of their followers they could bring to the grudge match.

On a winter night in 1903, Eastman and Kelly arrived at a barn in the Bronx, ready to duke it out. About 50 gang members from each side gathered to watch the match and lend support to their respective leader. The two combatants entered the ring. Kelly's experience as a one-time bantamweight boxer gave him an edge in the fight's early rounds, but Eastman was bigger and tougher.

Both men fought hard, fully aware of the stakes. Their very reputations and the power of their gangs hinged on the outcome of the match. The fight dragged on . . . and on. After two hours, the leaders were lying across one another, still trying feebly to hit each other. Finally, the match was pronounced a draw. The fighters were loaded into carriages and brought back to their respective territories.

Though Monk Eastman did not lose to Paul Kelly that night, his days as a gang leader were numbered. Unlike Kelly, he was a loose cannon, and this caused his political patrons great consternation. On February 2, 1904, Eastman finally went too far. At around three o'clock that morning, he and an associate named Chris Wallace were on their way to rough up someone who had been giving one of the gang's clients trouble when they spotted a well-dressed man staggering drunkenly down the street near Times Square. They also noticed that this man was being followed by an unsavory-looking character. Eastman and Wallace assumed the drunk was about to be robbed.

Wanting to get a jump on the action, they walked over to the lush and stuck their guns under his nose. As their fingers reached for the man's pockets, the unsavory-looking character began firing his gun at them. It turned out that the drunk was a wealthy young man and his shadow was a Pinkerton detective who had been assigned to protect him. Eastman and Wallace shot back at the detective and then fled. However, as they looked over their shoulders to check on their pursuer, they inadvertently ran straight into a police-man. Somehow, Wallace managed to escape, but the police-man caught Eastman and clubbed him into unconsciousness with his nightstick. The gang leader was arrested and tossed into a cell at the police station on West 30th Street. Two days later, he was indicted for robbery and felonious assault.

At first, Eastman was amused at the turn of events. It wasn't like he'd be spending too much time behind bars. His political allies would surely make the charges go away — or so he thought. But the seriousness of his situation began to sink in when Tammany Hall politicians wouldn't respond to his pleas for help. They'd cut him loose, and now he was on his own. There were no more Tammany bondsmen or lawyers to bail him out.

Eastman's trial got underway on April 12, 1904. He claimed he'd been trying to protect the young drunk from the unsavory character following him, and that he'd had no intention of committing a robbery. Not surprisingly, nobody bought his story. After one hour and 15 minutes of jury deliberation, Eastman was found guilty and sentenced to 10 years in prison. On April 23, he climbed into a van and was transferred to Sing Sing.

Eastman's lieutenants, Kid Twist and Ritchie Fitzpatrick, took over the gang when their leader went to prison. However, the power sharing didn't last long. In the fall of 1904, Kid Twist proposed a meeting at the Chrystie Street bar to discuss the gang's leadership. Fitzpatrick agreed. He arrived at the bar on November 1 and went straight to the back room. When someone suddenly turned off the lights, Fitzpatrick realized he'd been set up. By the time police arrived on the scene, the only thing they found was Fitzpatrick's body. He'd been shot through the heart and his arms had been carefully folded across his chest.

Kid Twist's sole leadership didn't last all that long, either. Shortly after Fitzpatrick was murdered, Kid Twist and Vach "Cyclone Louie" Lewis got into a barroom brawl with Five

Pointer Louis "the Lump" Pioggi. They were fighting over a woman whom both Twist and Pioggi admired. The Lump broke his ankle when he was forced to escape the skirmish by jumping out a second-story window. On May 14, 1908, Paul Kelly retaliated. The leader of the Five Points Gang had one of his thugs shoot Kid Twist to death outside a Coney Island bar. Badly demoralized by Twist's murder, the Eastman Gang broke into warring factions.

Meanwhile, Monk Eastman did his time at Sing Sing. When he was released on parole in June 1909, he returned to the East Side but never regained his former status as a gang leader. In 1912, a group of cops broke into Eastman's room and arrested him for smoking opium. This time, he was jailed for eight months. Almost immediately after his release in 1915, he was arrested for robbery and served nearly three years in Dannemora prison. In 1917, he joined the 106th Infantry of the New York National Guard under the name William Delaney, went to France, and distinguished himself.

Upon his return, Eastman went drinking one night with a few friends. Among them was Jerry Bohan, a corrupt Prohibition enforcement agent with whom Eastman was involved in a bootlegging operation. They arrived at the Blue Bird Cafe around midnight, where they drank and sang into the wee hours of the morning. At around 4 a.m., Eastman and Bohan left the bar and began to argue. Drunk and angry, Bohan pulled out a gun and fired at his business partner five times. Eastman collapsed. His bullet-riddled body was found on the sidewalk in front of the Blue Bird Cafe on December 26, 1920. He was buried with full military honors at Brooklyn's Cypress Hill Cemetery, and his old comrades from the 106th Infantry covered the cost of his funeral. Bohan was tried and convicted of murder.

Monk Eastman's longtime archrival outlived him by several years. In 1905, Paul Kelly survived an assassination attempt by his former lieutenant, James "Biff" Ellison. The ambitious Ellison had left the Five Points Gang and joined the Gophers. One evening, Ellison and Gopher member Razor Riley entered the New Brighton Dance Hall and spotted Kelly and fellow Five Pointer Bill Harrington sitting at a table at the back of the hall. As the two Gophers approached, Harrington shouted a warning to his leader. Razor Riley aimed his gun at Harrington and pulled the trigger. In the meantime, Kelly had managed to duck under the table. He re-emerged firing. In the ensuing gun battle, three bullets hit Kelly, and the would-be assassins fled. By the time police arrived on the scene, all that remained for them was Bill Harrington's body, lying in a pool of his own blood. The wounded Kelly had managed to stumble out of the dance hall.

Although Paul Kelly outlasted Monk Eastman as a gang leader, he began losing his grip on power during the month he was recovering from his wounds. Membership in the Five Points Gang dropped over the next few years, as did the gang's importance. Kelly saw the writing on the wall. He moved his business headquarters to Harlem, where he became a real estate broker and a business agent for unions.

The fierce rivalry between the Eastman Gang and the Five Points Gang had finally fizzled out, but violent clashes between other New York gangs would continue to be a part of the area's landscape for some time.

Chapter 4
The Tong Wars

Mock Duck squatted on his haunches in the middle of the street, closed his eyes, and squeezed the triggers of both his .45 revolvers simultaneously as he pivoted in a full circle on the balls of his feet. A notoriously poor shot, the leader of the Hip Sing Tong was nevertheless feared throughout Chinatown for his fighting technique because he was dangerous to anyone within range of his weapons. Bullets would simply spray the enemies around him.

Chinatown, an inner city neighborhood on the Lower East Side, was a small, crowded area wedged between the Five Points and the Bowery. The majority of its residents were men who had come to the United States to make money and send it back to their wives and families in China. The Chinese

Exclusion Act of 1882 kept women out of the country.

Chinatown's population grew steadily throughout the late 1800s, and Chinese businesses sprang up on Mott Street in the little block between Pell Street and Chatham Square. They included basement boardinghouses, a grocer, a tailor, and New York's first Chinese restaurant. Despite the success of these businesses, Chinese residents were largely isolated from the rest of society by their culture and language. This isolation prompted the organization of benevolent associations that united and supported Chinese members, providing them with aid and advice when needed, and protecting their personal and business interests.

The smaller of these associations were called tongs, which, roughly translated, means "meeting halls." Belonging to a tong became a way for Chinese immigrants to get ahead in a society in which anti-Chinese economic and social policies blocked opportunities for social advancement. Some of the tongs were involved in criminal activities such as gambling, prostitution, and opium trafficking.

The first tong to be established in New York City was the On Leong Tong. In 1883, Tom Lee, the leader of the On Leongs, bought a building on Mott Street and turned it into the tong's headquarters. From there, the On Leongs ran a lucrative empire of gambling houses, brothels, and opium dens. Throughout the 1880s and 1890s, Lee's organization ruled Chinatown with virtually no opposition. The local police were paid to turn a blind eye to the On Leongs' illegal activities. Meanwhile, Tom Lee's political patrons called him the "Mayor of Chinatown," and he personally controlled the six votes that were assigned to the Chinese community in elections of any sort. When he was made a deputy sheriff of New York County, the diminutive Lee took to wandering around Chinatown wearing a silver star on his chain-mail shirt and walking everywhere with either hand resting on a bodyguard's shoulder.

In the spring of 1899, the ambitious Mock Duck arrived on the scene and changed everything for Lee. Originally named Sai Wing Mock, the 20-year-old Mock Duck was a known gambler, and word quickly spread throughout Chinatown that the newcomer would bet on anything, including whether an orange picked at random from a fruit cart had an odd or even number of seeds.

Shortly after his arrival in New York, Mock Duck aligned himself with the Hip Sing Tong, a rival gang of the On Leongs. The Hip Sings had gotten their start in the early 1890s, when a few families had banded together for protection from other organizations. Compared to the On Leongs, the Hip Sings held little power in New York's Chinatown — that is, until Mock Duck came along. He made it clear very quickly that he was both courageous and determined.

One day, not long after Mock Duck joined the Hip Sings, a fellow tong member went to a tenement on Mott Street, in On Leong territory, to visit a cousin — a dangerous undertaking given the ever-present hostilities between the two tongs. Upon hearing about the presence of an enemy in their midst, the On Leongs dispatched some of their members to stake out the tenement and attack the Hip Sing member as soon as he emerged. As the On Leong members waited for their quarry to appear, word of the standoff reached Hip Sing headquarters. Agreeing that their man had been a fool to go into enemy territory in the first place, the Hip Sings' council decided he would have to fend for himself.

But Mock Duck could not abandon his poor colleague. Calmly, he walked over to Mott Street by himself, knowing full well that members of the rival tong could easily shoot him if they wanted to. Making his way past the On Leongs who were camped out in front of the tenement, he called on his associate trapped inside to come out. The man obliged. The On Leongs, either out of shock at Mock Duck's audacity or respect for his boldness, did nothing as the two Hip Sings escaped back to safe territory.

Not long after that incident, Mock Duck took over leadership of the Hip Sing Tong. Within a year he had greatly increased its membership, and, inevitably, tensions with the On Leongs began to grow.

Mock Duck was aware that Tom Lee and the On Leongs were raking in substantial profits from their gambling dens, and he wanted a piece of the action. Realizing he needed some leverage to make this happen, he knew just who to turn to for help: Reverend Charles H. Parkhurst, president of the Society for the Prevention of Crime. Years earlier, on February

14, 1892, Reverend Parkhurst of the Madison Square Church had delivered a fierce sermon about crime in New York. This sermon, which had described the rampant political and police corruption in the city, had made newspaper headlines and shocked many New Yorkers. To substantiate his claims, Parkhurst had hired a detective who had taken him on a tour of "sin city." Dressed in disguises, the pair had visited saloons, gambling houses, opium dens, and whorehouses. A month after his startling sermon, Parkhurst had sworn out an affidavit of what he had seen. Following this, two committees (Lexow in 1894 and Mazet in 1897) went on to investigate crime and corruption in the city.

Now, more than eight years after he delivered his damning sermon, Parkhurst was leading a group of local reformers who were bent on publicizing the graft and corruption throughout New York City. Mock Duck saw an opportunity to use Parkhurst's reform movement to further his own ambitions — and he seized it.

The Hip Sings developed an alliance with Parkhurst's organization against the On Leong Tong. They met with Frank Moss, a former president of the New York Police Board who acted as legal counsel to the Society for the Prevention of Crime. The Hip Sings convinced Moss that their tong was reform-minded. They explained that, just as Moss wanted to rid New York of crime and corruption, they wanted to do the same for Chinatown. And, while Moss was fighting Tammany Hall and the corrupt police force in his quest to clean up the city, they were up against the powerful and corrupt On Leongs. They convinced Moss that the Society for the Prevention of Crime should work with the Hip Sings since they were, after all, on the same side. Moss agreed.

This new partnership gave Mock Duck an ace up his sleeve. If he couldn't get Tom Lee to grant the Hip Sings a piece of the gambling action in Chinatown, Mock Duck would start giving Moss the addresses of On Leong gambling places. Inevitably, these illegal operations would be raided and closed down by the police. Once this happened, the Hip Sings could move in and set up their own games of chance.

His relationship with Moss and Parkhurst firmly established, Mock Duck went to see Tom Lee. In a respectful voice, he proposed a 50-50 split of Chinatown's gambling profits. Not surprisingly, the leader of the On Leongs laughed at the proposal — he wasn't interested.

On July 21, 1904, the Society for the Prevention of Crime staged its first raids on gambling houses controlled by the On Leong Tong. Society members visited six dens on Pell, Mott, and Doyers Streets. Soon after the houses were closed down, they were reopened under Hip Sing control. Lee protested to Parkhurst and Moss, but to no avail. The two members of the Society for the Prevention of Crime were unwittingly helping Mock Duck in his plans to undermine the On Leongs. The Hip Sing leader later replaced the private altar in the tong's headquarters with a huge crayon portrait of Frank Moss.

A few weeks after the first raids were carried out on their

gambling dens, the On Leongs' boardinghouse on Pell Street burned down, killing two tong members. Mock Duck insisted he knew nothing about the fire. Nevertheless, he now had Tom Lee's attention — and the run of Pell Street. Not long afterwards, the two tongs declared war on each other.

Traditionally, before two tongs went to war they would post a declaration of their intentions (a *chun hung*) on walls throughout the community. Then each side would mobilize its salaried soldiers, known as "hatchetmen" or "highbinders." These men usually wore chain-mail shirts and armed themselves with hatchets and revolvers. A tong war could go on for weeks, months, or even years.

At the start of the war between the On Leongs and the Hip Sings, Bayard Street and Mott Street were under On Leong control. Pell Street, meanwhile, belonged to the Hip Sings. Tong members conducted their business solely within their own territory. If they stepped out of that territory to do business, battles resulted.

With On Leong headquarters on Mott Street and Hip Sing headquarters on Pell Street, that left Doyers Street the no man's land of the tong war. A sharp bend in this crooked street earned the nickname the "Bloody Angle." Many men were murdered there because it was the perfect spot for an ambush — it was virtually impossible to see around the corner.

As the battles between the two tongs raged on, the On Leongs realized that Mock Duck was truly a force to be reckoned with. He hadn't been kidding when he'd told Lee that he would fight for half the gambling privileges in Chinatown. Watching his power and control ebb away, Tom Lee was out for revenge: he put a $1000 bounty on Mock Duck's head. At 1:30 a.m. on November 3, 1904, Mock Duck was climbing the basement stairs at Hip Sing headquarters when three On Leong members suddenly appeared. They squatted, closed their eyes, and started shooting. Mock Duck crumpled to the ground. He'd been hit in the stomach.

Upon hearing the sound of gunfire, police officers in the area rushed to Hip Sing headquarters. By the time they arrived on the scene, two of the gunmen had fled. The officers encircled the third man, Lee Sing, creating a protective wall around him. Then they moved as a unit, advancing toward Chatham Square and a waiting patrol wagon. Hip Sings surrounded them, waving hatchets and pistols and desperately looking for a crack in the gunman's human shield. They were determined to get revenge for Mock Duck's shooting. Somehow the police managed to push the gunman into the safety of the patrol wagon.

To the disappointment of the On Leongs, Mock Duck survived the attack. He spent almost three weeks in Hudson Hospital and was released on November 22. He then spent his time convalescing at Hip Sing headquarters with round-the-clock bodyguards watching over him. Mock Duck knew he was an easy target in his weakened state. He was certain the On Leongs would try again to kill him — particularly since he was set to testify against his assailant the following week. Even the merchants in the area sensed the impending attack. They closed up shop to avoid getting caught in the inevitable crossfire. Meanwhile, local policemen took up posts throughout Chinatown after being tipped off that another assassination attempt was in the works.

Despite the heightened state of alert in the neighborhood, members of the On Leong Tong managed to sneak over to Hip Sing headquarters. Mock Duck's bodyguards, however, were ready for the invasion and managed to protect their leader in the ensuing exchange of gunfire. The attackers quickly took off.

Soon after the incident, the Hip Sings plastered Chinatown's buildings with signs offering $3000 for the murder of Tom Lee. Lee went to the police, who provided officers to protect him. Skirmishes between the two tongs continued and escalated, as did the raids on gambling establishments in Chinatown. Meanwhile, neighborhood residents cautiously carried on with their everyday lives.

At that time, people from all over Chinatown took in shows at the Chinese Theater on Doyers Street. Patrons regularly filled the theater, happy to sit surrounded by the lush decor and watch performances that transported them back to their homeland. Among these patrons were the members of the On Leong Tong — Tom Lee and his men enjoyed the opera and could usually be found in the basement theater most Sunday nights.

On August 6, 1905, patrons at the Chinese Theater were

enjoying another popular Sunday night show when, just after 10 p.m., a member of the Hip Sings interrupted the performance by lighting firecrackers at the front of the theater. Suddenly, other members of Mock Duck's gang stood up and began firing their .44 revolvers at members of the On Leong Tong sitting in the audience. The Hip Sings had strategically placed themselves in the front and the back rows of the auditorium, sandwiching their rivals in the middle. Panic and pandemonium broke out. Some On Leongs tried to head for the exits only to discover that their enemies had blocked the escape routes, trapping theatergoers inside. The On Leong men drew their weapons and returned fire as actors, musicians, and innocent audience members dove for cover.

While terrified witnesses cowered beneath their seats, police rushed to the tiny theater from all over the Lower East Side, using their clubs to beat their way through the crowd that had converged outside. By the time they got to the scene of the shootout, four On Leongs were dead and another 20 had been injured. The police arrested 20 people, a number of whom were affiliated with the Hip Sing Tong. Others involved in the shootout managed to escape, dragging their wounded comrades through underground passageways that led from the theater. Mock Duck was found later that night, hiding in a building in the Bowery. He was promptly arrested and accused of orchestrating the ambush, despite the fact that he had an alibi. At the time of the shootout, he had been at the police station bailing out some Hip Sing gamblers who had been arrested. The following day, he was released on $1000 bail and did not serve jail time.

Murders and ambushes continued, and the police became increasingly concerned about the ongoing violence in Chinatown. On January 31, 1906, Judge Warren W. Foster of the Court of General Sessions brought the two tongs together in the presence of Chinese diplomatic representatives. Foster invited Tom Lee and Mock Duck to his house and got both leaders to agree to a truce. He convinced them to sign a peace treaty that laid out the terms of their agreement: the On Leongs would rule Mott Street, the Hip Sings would dominate Pell Street, and Doyers Street would be neutral territory.

The truce was toasted at a dinner, but the celebrations were short-lived. Within a week, the archrivals were at it again. This time the war was set off when a Hip Sing gunman shot an On Leong member in the Bloody Angle of Doyers Street. Six months later, Judge Foster succeeded in getting the tong leaders to sign another treaty. It lasted until 1909, which was to become the bloodiest year of the tong war.

The next round of hostilities was triggered by the murder of a young woman named Bow Kum, also known as Little Sweet Flower. Years earlier, Bow Kum's father had sold her into slavery in Canton, China. She was shipped to San Francisco, where a man named Low Hee Tong bought her for $3000. Low Hee Tong was a member of the Four Brothers, an ally of the Hip Sings. The couple lived together for four years, until the police took her away when Low Hee Tong couldn't produce a marriage certificate. Bow Kum was then placed in a Christian mission, where she fell in love with a gardener by the name of Tchin Len, who happened to be a member of the On Leong Tong. Tchin Len married Bow Kum and brought her to New York. Upon hearing this news, Low Hee Tong tried to persuade the gardener to return the $3000 he had spent on Bow Kum, but Tchin Len refused.

Angered, Low Hee Tong sent a letter to the Four Brothers and Hip Sings in New York explaining the situation and asking for redress. The tong leaders discussed it and agreed that Low Hee Tong had a point. They approached the On Leong Tong and asked that Low Hee Tong be reimbursed. The request was ignored, and the Hip Sings went to war again. Posters in violent colors appeared on billboards throughout the community. Then, on August 15, 1909, someone slipped into Tchin Len's home on Mott Street, stabbed Bow Kum in the heart, and slit her throat. This set off a bloodbath that would result in about 50 deaths, many more wounded, and property destroyed by the bombs the Chinese gangs had begun using as part of their warfare.

As the tong battles raged on, comedian Ah Hoon, a member of the On Leongs, interspersed his performances at the Chinese Theater with humorous commentaries on activities in Chinatown. Being an On Leong man, he directed many of his barbs at the Hip Sings and their allies, the Four Brothers. Although warned by Reverend Huie Kim, head of the Morning Star Mission on Doyers Street, that he was playing with fire,

Ah Hoon continued with his act. Inevitably, this made him a marked man in the eyes of the Hip Sings. Wanting to give the comedian fair warning about his demise, they sent a messenger to tell him when and where he'd be murdered. The messenger informed Ah Hoon that he would be killed on the very stage from which he'd made his insulting comments.

On December 30, 1909, Ah Hoon's neighbor went to the police and asked them to protect the comedian during his performance that night. Chief Inspector Sergeant John D. Coughlin and two patrolmen accompanied Ah Hoon to the theater. Their blue uniforms looked strangely out of place as they sat on the stage during the show.

Ah Hoon, terrified by the death threat, trembled with fear during his performance and avoided making any jokes about the Hip Sings and Four Brothers. Though word of the Hip Sings' intentions had gotten around, Ah Hoon nevertheless performed to a full house. Outside the building, a large crowd had gathered to see what would happen. They had been unable to buy even standing-room tickets to the show.

As it turned out, the police presence intimidated the Hip Sing gunmen, who didn't end up killing Ah Hoon onstage that night. When the show was over, the officers escorted the frightened comedian through an underground passageway to his home on Chatham Square. He locked his door and went to bed. As he slept, heavily armed On Leong men stood guard in the doorway of his house while others patrolled the surrounding streets.

Despite the added security, Ah Hoon's neighbor discovered the comedian's dead body the next morning. A Hip Sing killer sitting in a boatswain's chair had been lowered from the roof and had shot the popular comedian through the window.

Hostilities between the two tongs intensified on New Year's Day. That evening, the Chinese Theater was filled with spectators who had come to enjoy the celebration of the year. A rumor had been circulating around Chinatown that the warring factions had declared a truce, and, as a result, audience members were able to relax enough to enjoy the performance. Suddenly, someone stood up and tossed a handful of lit firecrackers into the air above a row of orchestra seats. As the firecrackers popped and cracked, members of the Hip Sings once again whipped out their pistols and began firing at the On Leongs in the audience. The crowd started to panic. It was apparent that rumors of a truce had been grossly exaggerated — the war between the tongs had not abated at all.

By the time the building was cleared, five On Leong men were dead. The police immediately suspected that the Hip Sings were responsible for the murders. They arrested several tong members but had to release them due to lack of evidence.

The owners of the Chinese Theater did not share the Hip Sings' good luck. The violent shootouts had been very bad for business. Though both tongs agreed to no longer carry out their battles inside the theater, they continued to hurt attendance by attacking their victims as they emerged from a show. Audiences at performances grew smaller as people became increasingly scared of being caught in the crossfire on Doyers Street. The theater finally closed its doors in 1910.

Fed up with the violence, the Chinese Consul in Washington set up a committee comprised mainly of Chinese merchants, teachers, and students to find a solution to the tong war. In late 1910, the committee managed to negotiate a truce between the tongs, but periodic skirmishes continued nonetheless.

Although Mock Duck had been repeatedly arrested over the years for murder and gambling, the police and prosecutors had never been able to make any of the charges stick. Then, finally, in 1912, Mock Duck was convicted of running a game of chance and was sent to Sing Sing. Upon his release he moved to Brooklyn, where he died of natural causes on July 24, 1941.

While Mock Duck was in prison, the Hip Sings persisted with their quest to kill Tom Lee — and nearly succeeded. On one occasion, they fired a bullet through Lee's window and shattered an alarm clock on a shelf beside his head. Despite the attempts on his life, Lee survived the tong wars and died a natural death in 1917 at the ripe old age of 76. By that time, the war between the On Leongs and the Hip Sings had all but ended.

Chapter 5
Corruption in Blue

Herman "Beansy" Rosenthal wasn't having much luck with his gambling business. In the early 1900s, operating a saloon, gambling house, or brothel in New York City meant having to pay off Tammany Hall politicians and members of the police department in order to avoid raids and prosecution. But Beansy wouldn't pay off anyone, and, as a result, he was always having problems with the police or with other gamblers.

Rosenthal had started his dubious career as a bookmaker at the racetracks. In 1910, he decided to open a gambling joint in Far Rockaway on Long Island. A rival who was worried about losing clients managed to get the police to raid Rosenthal's place so many times that Beansy had to close it down. He then opened the Hesper Club on Second Avenue. That business quickly failed because of strong competition from Louis "Bridgie" Webber's Sans Souci Music Hall, which was located nearby on Third Avenue. Undeterred, Rosenthal opened another gambling house on West 116th Street. It, too, was closed down by police. His next effort was a joint on West 45th Street. That place was raided repeatedly and firebombed twice.

Around this time, New York City's main gambling district extended north from West 33rd Street on either side of Broadway to 59th Street. Most of the gambling joints in the district received official protection. Businesses that included roulette and faro had to pay $500 to open their doors and then make monthly payments of $300 to police in order to operate with impunity. Gambling house owners in the area also forged close relationships with gang leaders in order to ensure protection. The gambling industry in New York City was flourishing, and violence — or fear of violence — was an integral part of its success.

Despite his numerous setbacks, Rosenthal decided to give the industry one more try. He figured his luck had changed for the better when he was introduced to Charles H. Becker, a lieutenant with the New York Police Department. The pair met in late 1911 at a ball hosted by the Order of Elks. They drank and chatted. Then they met again at the Elks Club on New Year's Eve. After a champagne-soaked evening, Becker threw his arm around Rosenthal and promised to grant any favor Rosenthal asked for.

As head of the vice squad, Lieutenant Becker was in a position to grant many favors. He was responsible for cleaning up New York by ridding the city of gambling, prostitution, and rowdyism. Becker reported directly to Police Commissioner Rhinelander Waldo, the city's eighth police commissioner in just eleven years. A former army officer who was seen as incorruptible, Waldo headed a department that was soaked in corruption. He was so naïve when it came to spotting treachery that he would allow policemen to investigate themselves whenever a complaint was lodged against them. Naturally, these officers were always exonerated.

Among the corrupt officers in the department, Lieutenant Becker was the "crookedest." Rather than eliminating vice, he used his power to shake down illegal businesses and line his own pockets. He topped up his meager policeman's salary by extorting money from prostitutes and owners of gaming houses. At a time when his yearly salary as a lieutenant was a mere $1687, Becker managed to deposit $58,845 into his savings account. There was no doubt he was prospering.

A large, physically imposing cop, Charles Becker was born in the Catskills in 1870 and moved to the Lower East Side when he was a teenager. As a young man, he held a number of menial jobs, including working as a bouncer at the Atlantic Gardens German beer hall. In 1893, he joined the police department, and it soon became clear that he had a penchant for brutality and a talent for getting into trouble.

On September 20, 1896, Becker stumbled upon three men robbing a tobacco store. He hit one man with his club, then he and his partner shot at the other two, killing one of them. The dead man, it turned out, was not a burglar at all, but a 19-year-old plumber's assistant who happened to be in the wrong place at the wrong time. Becker was suspended for a month. A few months later, a teenager accused Becker of beating him senseless in the lobby of a theater.

The trouble did not end there. In 1904, Becker saved a man who had fallen off a Hudson River pier. The police department awarded him its highest honor for heroism. Two years later, however, the "rescued" man alleged that Becker had reneged on a promise to pay him for "falling" into the water. It appeared that Becker's heroic act was a setup to polish his tarnished reputation.

Becker first learned how to top up his small policeman's salary by watching his boss do the same. Captain Max Schmittberger was a corrupt cop who demanded money from saloons, gambling joints, brothels, and other illegal operations. When Becker learned that Schmittberger was earning $300 a month in protection money, he wanted a piece of the action. He walked into a gambling joint on West 38th Street and demanded that the owner pay him $20 a month, in addition to the $300 he was already paying Schmittberger. The man complied. Surprised at how easy his first take had been, he was soon collecting protection money everywhere he went.

Word of Becker's initiative got back to Schmittberger, who promptly summoned the young officer to his office and demanded the money that he'd collected the day before. Once the money was handed over, Schmittberger made Becker his bagman, responsible for collecting protection money every month in exchange for a 10 percent commission.

Then, in 1910, Commissioner Waldo created three "strong arm" vice squads to clean up the city. He assigned Becker to head one of these squads, putting the officer in a prime position to collect graft. If any of the city's gambling house operators didn't want to pay Becker a bribe to protect their establishments, he simply raided their businesses. These raids showed his bosses just how diligent he was about cleaning up the city, but they also sent a message to those gamblers who were reluctant to pony up. Becker even hired a publicity agent to promote his achievements on the right side of the law. But while the publicity agent was touting his honorable accomplishments, Becker was collecting kickbacks from illicit business operators.

Becker soon grew so busy that he needed his own bagman. He hired Bald Jack Rose — a gambler, prizefight promoter, and one-time minor league baseball manager — to be his main collector. Meanwhile, the current leader of the Eastman Gang, Big Jack Zelig, was hired as muscle. If a police raid wasn't enough to convince the owner of a gambling house to cooperate with Becker, Big Jack Zelig could often be relied on to beat the owner into submission. With Rose and Zelig on his team, dirty money was simply flowing into Becker's pockets.

In early 1912, Lieutenant Becker decided to sign on as Beansy Rosenthal's silent partner in Rosenthal's latest gambling venture. It sounded like a good arrangement to Rosenthal. After all, having a policeman for a partner would keep the place from getting raided. For reasons that nobody could explain, Rosenthal also had the support and protection of Tammany Hall politician Big Tim Sullivan, which certainly didn't hurt. Sullivan had lent Rosenthal $2000 to open the business, sparking rumors that the politician was also a partner in the gambling house. Becker, meanwhile, contributed a $1500 loan, but it came with strings attached. Rosenthal had to take Jack Rose in as Becker's representative and pay him 25 percent of the profits. Not having much of a choice in the matter, Rosenthal agreed to the terms, and the gambling house opened its doors in mid-town Manhattan in February 1912.

The peace and stability that Rosenthal craved for his latest business venture didn't last long. Relations between Becker and Rosenthal began to sour less than a month later, when Rosenthal refused to contribute $500 towards the defense fund of Becker's publicity agent, Charlie Plitt. Plitt had been charged with killing a man during a raid on a dice game, and Becker had requested that each gambling outfit in the district make a donation to the press agent's defense.

By this time, Big Tim Sullivan was losing his mental

faculties due to an inflammation of the brain brought on by syphilis. As a result of his condition, he was also losing clout in Tammany Hall. Sullivan was no longer in a position to protect Rosenthal — and Becker knew it. When Beansy persisted in his refusal to contribute to Plitt's defense, Becker sent Jack Zelig's men to beat him up. But even after the beating, Rosenthal still refused to pay the $500.

Meanwhile, Police Commissioner Waldo was beginning to wonder why Rosenthal's gambling joint had never been raided. It seemed suspicious to the commissioner that this particular gambling house would remain untouched while other joints were being raided on a regular basis. Becker was suddenly under pressure to take action. In order to appease his boss and keep from looking guilty, he had no choice but to raid the very joint he had a stake in.

Becker sent Bald Jack Rose to ask Rosenthal if he would agree to a "friendly" raid. Over the years, Becker had overseen a number of these raids, all of which were carried out to appease the public's demand for an end to gambling operations. Although a gambling joint was always closed down after a friendly raid, it would quietly reopen once public attention died down. Nevertheless, Rosenthal was angered by the request and refused to play along. After all, he had agreed to take Becker on as a partner in order to *avoid* being raided. He'd endured too many attacks on his gambling joints in the past and saw this as just more police harassment.

Becker was irritated by Rosenthal's lack of cooperation.

Given the pressure he was feeling from the police commissioner and the public, the lieutenant had little choice but to carry on with his plan. On April 15, 1912, he led his squad on a raid of Rosenthal's gambling house — and it was anything but friendly. Wanting to punish his defiant business partner, Becker had police posted in front of Rosenthal's joint 24 hours a day to keep it closed.

Rosenthal felt he'd been double-crossed. He was determined to retaliate and threatened to squeal on Becker. He warned that he would sing like a canary to the district attorney that the head of the vice squad was his business partner and was also running protection rackets to keep the police out of certain illicit establishments.

Other gamblers started to worry. If Rosenthal opened his mouth, it could spell the end of the gambling business and cost illegal operators a lot of money. Gangster Arnold Rothstein offered Rosenthal $500 to leave town and lie low for a while, but the stubborn Beansy refused.

Gamblers weren't the only ones concerned. Becker was worried, too. His career would be over if word got out that he was working with a gambler and that he'd been shaking down operators. Rosenthal was proving to be a liability, and Becker needed to eliminate this threat permanently. It was time to talk to his "muscle" man, Big Jack Zelig.

Of all the gang leaders who were working with gambling house owners at the time, Big Jack Zelig was the most powerful. His services were invaluable. Not only did he supply his clients with rock-solid protection, he would also blackjack their business rivals. It was rumored that some gambling house owners paid Zelig large amounts of money just to keep his men away from their establishments.

In June 1912, while Becker was fretting over his escalating feud with Rosenthal, Zelig was cooling his heels in the Tombs jail. He'd been tossed in the slammer on a false charge of concealing a weapon. Eager to solve the Rosenthal problem as quickly as possible, Becker sent Bald Jack Rose to the Tombs to talk to the gang leader. Zelig was promised his freedom in exchange for supplying the gunmen to bump off Rosenthal. He was also offered $2000 to pay these gunmen.

Zelig agreed to the offer and was released from jail. He promptly tracked down four gunmen who had worked for him in the past: Harry "Gyp the Blood" Horowitz, Louis "Lefty Louie" Rosenberg, Frank "Dago Frank" Cirofici, and Jacob "Whitey Lewis" Seidenshner. Gyp the Blood was the leader of the Lenox Avenue Gang, which consisted of a small group of burglars and pickpockets, but he was also loyal to the Eastman Gang and would work for them whenever Zelig required his help. Particularly talented at beating people up, Gyp the Blood could, allegedly, break a man's back over his knee. The other hit men were also known for specific talents. Lefty Louis was an excellent pickpocket, Dago Frank was a skilled gunman, and Whitey Lewis was a blackjack artist.

The foursome planned to carry out the hit on Rosenthal in early July 1912. Initially, their idea was to kill him while he was eating dinner with his wife at the Garden Cafe. But for some reason, they chickened out.

Rosenthal, meanwhile, was still feeling chatty. On July 13, he went to the office of the *New York World* newspaper and swore out an affidavit that Becker was his partner and had taken 20 percent of the profits of his gambling house. When the statement was published in the newspaper the next day, District Attorney Charles S. Whitman immediately summoned Rosenthal to his office.

After a five-hour meeting with Whitman, Rosenthal agreed to make a complete statement to a New York County grand jury the following morning. He left the district attorney's office at 11 p.m. and headed out for a late dinner and drinks. Whitman had told him to stay home and lie low, but Rosenthal had a mind of his own. At midnight, he walked into the restaurant at the Hotel Metropole on 43rd Street and grabbed a table. He ate a big steak dinner and downed a few drinks as a ragtime piano player tickled the ivories.

After nearly two hours had passed, an acquaintance walked over to Rosenthal's table and told him that someone wanted to see him outside. Rosenthal got up, paid his bill, and left a generous tip. He put on his hat and left the restaurant. On his way out of the hotel, Rosenthal picked up several morning newspapers to take a look; his name was splashed across the front pages. Pleased at the sight, Rosenthal stepped outside the hotel and onto the street off Times Square. As he paused on the steps, four men leapt from a car and opened fire at point blank range. Three bullets hit Rosenthal in the head, ripping off the left side of his face. A fourth got him in the neck. Rosenthal dropped to the ground and died instantly. It was 1:56 a.m. — about eight hours before Rosenthal was scheduled to appear before the grand jury to tell them everything he knew about Becker and his rackets.

In a flash, the gunmen stuffed themselves back into the car and made their getaway. But they had been sloppy. Cabaret singer Charles Gallagher happened to be walking past the hotel when Rosenthal was gunned down. He made a note of the getaway car's license plate number and gave it to police.

Meanwhile, District Attorney Whitman was alerted that his star witness had been murdered. He rushed to the West 47th Street police station to take charge of the investigation. Becker was already at the station when Whitman arrived, and the district attorney found it odd that the lieutenant would be there at such a late hour. As it turned out, Jack Rose had called his boss from a telephone booth in the Times Building to let Becker know about the murder. Becker had then made his way down to the station house to see Beansy's body for himself.

Whitman realized too late that he should have provided protection to Rosenthal. Under the circumstances, however, police protection would have been out of the question. Thanks to Gallagher's tip, Whitman quickly discovered that the getaway car was a 1909 gray Packard driven by a man named William Shapiro. The car's owner was Louis Libby, who would rent it out for hire, but his partner, Shapiro, was the one who had driven it that night.

Once Whitman tracked Shapiro down, Shapiro admitted that he had driven the getaway car for the hit men and that Becker's bagman, Bald Jack Rose, had hired him. Shapiro claimed to have been unaware of the true plan, saying that he thought the thugs were only going to beat up Rosenthal — not kill him. He then gave police the names of the men he'd chauffeured: Gyp the Blood Horowitz, Lefty Louie Rosenberg, Dago Frank Cirofici, and Whitey Lewis Seidenshner. Armed with Shapiro's information, it didn't take long for Whitman to figure out that Becker was behind the hit.

Details of Rosenthal's murder were soon broadcast on the radio. Jack Rose went to police headquarters a few days after the killing and surrendered, perhaps believing that he might be able to negotiate a deal that would keep him out of jail in exchange for divulging details about Becker's plan. By the time Becker was arrested on July 29, the police had gamblers Harry Vallon, Bridgie Webber, and Sam Schepps in custody. These men had been with Rose the night of the murder and became police informants. They told detectives all about Becker's plot to have Beansy Rosenthal murdered. Like Shapiro, they also provided the names of the four gunmen.

Zelig, meanwhile, was conveniently out of town, as he had been when the hit had taken place. He was picked up in Providence, Rhode Island, and sent back to New York for questioning. Rose, Webber, and Vallon were kept as witnesses against Becker, and Libby and Shapiro gained immunity as material witnesses to the killing.

The hunt to find the hit men was also underway. On July 25, 1912, the police received a tip that Dago Frank was hiding out in a flat in Harlem. They raided the place and found him, and two companions, in an opium stupor. A week later, Whitey Lewis was caught in Kingston, just as he was boarding a train headed for Chicago. Gyp the Blood and Lefty Louis, however, were still on the lam, and they remained so for nearly two months.

It was their wives who inadvertently revealed their whereabouts. Detectives had been following the women, hoping that they would lead them to the fugitives. Finally, one of the wives made the grievous mistake of talking about the location of the hideout a little too loudly. Detectives quickly set up a stakeout at a building on Woodward Avenue in Queens and waited. On September 14, they watched as Lefty Louis's wife walked into the building and went up to an apartment to see her husband. The police officers followed her, treading lightly down the hall towards the apartment. With guns drawn, they kicked in the door. The two remaining hit men, their wives, and another man were taken by surprise. The women screamed.

Gyp the Blood and Lefty Louis knew the jig was up. Neither of them put up a fight. Their only request was that they be allowed to change out of their casual clothes and into expensive suits before heading to the police station. Gyp the Blood was annoyed at not having a hat to wear, so one of the detectives loaned him his until they reached the station. The four gunmen were charged in connection with the Rosenthal killing, and it was believed that Zelig would be called as a witness in Becker's trial.

On October 4, 1912, just days before he was scheduled to deliver his testimony, Zelig attended a party at the Stuyvesant Casino. While he was there, he got into an argument with a small-time hood by the name of Red Phil Davidson. The next day, Zelig was sitting in Siegel's Cafe when Davidson sent a messenger inside to ask Zelig to meet him outside. Zelig refused. Davidson waited around for a while and then went inside and told Zelig he wanted to borrow three dollars, and also that he wanted to be friends. Though both requests seemed a little strange, Zelig agreed. Then Davidson went back outside and continued to hang around the area.

A short while later, Zelig left the cafe and hopped on a streetcar heading north. Davidson chased the streetcar for one or two blocks and then jumped aboard. He walked towards Zelig, who was sitting near the front of the car. When Davidson got close enough, he aimed his .38-caliber revolver and fired, hitting the leader of the Eastman Gang behind the left ear. Zelig let out a small cry, grabbed the back of his head, and slumped forward. He died almost instantly.

Davidson was quickly caught and arrested. He initially tried to make it look like he had killed Zelig over the fight they'd had at the casino the previous night, claiming Zelig had stolen money from him. However, the pistol that Davidson had used in the killing was traced back to the police department. Although never proved, it was suspected that Becker had ordered the hit on Zelig to silence him before he testified at the lieutenant's trial.

Even without Zelig's testimony, there was still enough evidence against Becker in the Rosenthal killing. Becker pleaded not guilty at his arraignment. During the trial, Bald Jack Rose testified that Becker had told him, "I don't want [Rosenthal] beat up. I could do that myself. I could have a warrant for any gambling house that he frequents and make a raid on that place and beat him up for resisting arrest or anything else ... Nothing for that man but taken off this earth. Have him murdered, cut his throat, dynamited, or anything."

The four gunmen and former police lieutenant were all found guilty and sentenced to death by electric chair. Rosenberg, Horowitz, Seidenshner, and Cirofici were executed at Sing Sing prison on April 13, 1914. Although Rosenberg was the first one scheduled to die, it was decided to send Cirofici to the chair first because he became hysterical when the guards came to get his friend. Rosenberg went next, followed by Seidenshner and Horowitz.

Becker was convicted of first-degree murder on October 24, 1912, and was sent to Sing Sing to await execution on December 12, just six weeks after being sentenced. He appealed the decision. On February 24, 1914, the New York State Court of Appeals granted him a new trial on the grounds that the presiding trial judge, John W. Goff, had made some prejudicial rulings. In his nearly four days of instructions to the jury, Goff had presented as fact each of the prosecution's allegations. Goff had also headed the Lexow Committee in its investigation of police corruption in 1894. Becker was euphoric at the turn of events. Perhaps this time he would be exonerated.

Judge Samuel Seabury was chosen to preside over the second trial, which was set to begin on May 5, 1914. Becker's defense attorney this time around was W. Bourke Cockran, a Tammany lawyer who had once demanded that Mayor McClellan adopt a policy of wide-open gambling and prostitution in the city.

As the trial got underway, people lined up to get seats in the packed courtroom, eager to watch the disgraced police lieutenant be retried for the murder of a gambler. But on May 22, 1914, Becker's second trial ended just as the first one had. After deliberating for less than two hours, a jury found Lieutenant Charles Becker guilty — again. He was scheduled to be executed on July 16, 1915.

More appeals were filed and the execution was delayed. Becker appealed for clemency in 1915, asking the governor to exercise his power to commute a death sentence to life in jail. Ironically, the governor of New York at this point was none other than Charles Whitman, the district attorney who had prosecuted Becker in the first place.

Becker's appeal for clemency was turned down. The disgraced police lieutenant had truly reached the end. Early on the morning of July 30, 1915, guards arrived at Becker's cell in Sing Sing and led him on his final walk. He was strapped into the electric chair and pumped with current. When authorities checked his pulse, they found that he was still breathing. It would take two more attempts before he was finally executed.

After Becker's death, his widow, Helen, had a silver plate attached to the top of his coffin. It was inscribed with the words "Charles Becker. Murdered July 30, 1915 by Governor Whitman." She later had it removed when Police Inspector Joseph A. Faurot convinced her that she could be prosecuted for criminal libel.

The case of Lieutenant Charles Becker revealed to the citizens of New York the shockingly close ties between the city's police, its gangs, and its politicians. With Becker's conviction, the gambling businesses that had once operated so openly and relied so heavily on police and political corruption were suddenly forced underground. The days of collusion between police and gangs were over, but the city's politicians would continue to maintain their ties with gangsters.

Chapter 6
Killer Madden and the Gopher Gang

Dennis J. Keating couldn't sleep. His tenants were making a racket again. They had been renting a couple of rooms in the upstairs part of his house for less than a week, and the neighbors were already complaining about the bickering, brawling, and drunken partying that was going on up there. Figuring it was time to do something about it, Keating sighed, climbed out of bed, and went to talk to his new tenants. He knocked at their door and a man opened it. Inside the main room, Owney Madden and his friend Tanner Smith were sitting at a table having a discussion, a bottle of whiskey between them. Six other men were lounging around the room, listening to a seventh play a tune on a piano.

Determined to get a good night's sleep, Keating looked

right at Madden and told him that neighbors were complaining about the noise. The men would have to keep quiet, Keating warned, or he would be forced to evict them. Madden smiled. "Mister, did you ever hear of Owney Madden?" he asked the landlord.

"Yes," Keating answered, his voice shaking.

"Well, mister, *I* am Owney Madden."

Keating stared, speechless, at the notorious leader of the Gophers, the most formidable gang in Hell's Kitchen. He'd heard all the stories about this young man, who was nicknamed "the Killer," but he hadn't realized until that moment that Madden was his tenant. Without uttering another word, Keating turned around and went back downstairs. Though the noise from his renters continued, he decided that reporting them to the police was a bad idea. The Gophers, he knew, weren't shy about taking revenge.

While Keating did his best to ignore the constant ruckus, his neighbors grew more and more frustrated. One night, a tenant in a nearby building decided he'd had enough of the commotion and called the police. A patrolman was sent to investigate the noise complaint. However, after coming face to face with Madden and realizing whom he was dealing with, he returned to the police station and asked the precinct captain, Sergeant O'Connell, for help. There was no way he was going to face off against Madden and his men alone. Soon, a squad of officers was heading over to Keating's house.

But Madden was ready for them. He and his men had

barricaded the doors to the apartment, piling furniture against them to prevent the police from busting in. When the authorities demanded that they open up, the gangsters replied with threats and curses. As Sergeant O'Connell began to bang his nightstick against the door, a bullet shattered the glass of a nearby window and just missed a policeman's head. "We'll shoot the gizzard out of any cop that tries to get in here!" cried Madden. The sergeant knew this wasn't an idle threat. He and his men pulled back and went around the corner to plan their next move.

After some discussion, O'Connell ordered two of his men to slip into the house through the back while the rest of his crew waited across the street from the front of the house. O'Connell then walked up to the front door and began to argue with Owney Madden and Tanner Smith. The other gang members crowded around to hear the heated exchange, leaving a back window unguarded.

With the distraction that O'Connell had created at the front door, the two patrolmen were able to crawl into the house through the back window without being noticed. They crept towards the front room, where all the gangsters were now gathered. Upon reaching the room, the officers began hitting the gang members with their clubs.

Madden and his men were stunned. They hadn't antici-pated this. In order to avoid being hit with the clubs, the gangsters were forced to move away from the front door. That's when the rest of O'Connell's squad made its move.

The officers ran across the street, broke down the door, and crashed through the barricade. Using their clubs, they rounded up the thugs, handcuffing all of them. Fifteen minutes later, the gang members were marched into the street and stuffed into a patrol wagon for the ride to the police station.

The next day, the underage Madden appeared in court. A judge lectured him and placed him under a $500 bond to keep the peace for six months. Madden's buddy Tanner Smith was also released. Smith didn't waste any time. He headed over to city hall to show off his bruises and get some sympathy. In a meeting with Mayor William J. Gaylor, Smith claimed that policemen had hit him and his friends with clubs while they were playing cards. The mayor publicly reprimanded the police and then implemented Order No. 7, which barred officers from using their clubs unless they were forced to do so in self-defense.

Other gangsters were pleased with Smith's accomplishment. They congratulated him for bringing about an order that was sure to make it more difficult for cops to apprehend them. Smith reveled in their appreciation. A year later, however, his luck ran out when he was tossed in jail for carrying a revolver. About two years after Order No. 7 was implemented, the city's new mayor, John Purroy Mitchel, repealed it.

Throughout all of this, Owney Madden and his Gophers continued to wreak havoc on New York's West Side. "The Killer" had come by his nickname honestly. Born in Liverpool, England, in 1892, Owen Victor Madden arrived in the United

States at the tender age of 11. His family settled in the slums of Hell's Kitchen, where young Madden soon hooked up with the Gophers, a predominantly Irish gang that earned its name because members would often hide out in cellars and basements.

Comprised of nearly 500 members, the Gophers controlled much of the neighborhood. Their territory stretched from 14th Street to 42nd Street, and from 7th Avenue to 11th Avenue. In the early 1900s, the gang made a lot of money robbing the freight cars and depots of the New York Central Railroad on 11th Avenue. Fed up with the constant attacks, the railroad company eventually created its own special police force in order to stop the Gophers. Many of the men recruited to this force were former policemen who had dealt ineffectively with members of the gang before. This time, however, they would have more success. They used clubs and firearms to match their adversaries. Within a few months, the Gophers had lost their edge and were forced to abandon their thieving ways.

Loyalty was in short supply among members of the Gophers. Over the years, they went through a number of leaders, including Newburg Gallagher, Marty Brennan, Stumpy Malarkey, Goo Goo Knox, One Lung Curran, and Happy Jack Mulraney. Mulraney earned his nickname because partial muscle paralysis had given his face a permanent grin that made him look like he was always laughing. In fact, he was an ill-tempered man who was very sensitive about his impairment. One day, his friend Paddy the Priest, owner of a 10th Avenue saloon, asked the gangster why he never laughed on the other side of his face. Happy Jack shot the saloonkeeper and robbed the till. He was subsequently jailed for the murder.

In 1910, a police sweep collared Gophers leaders Gallagher and Brennan. The loss of the two latest leaders left the gang muddled and disorganized, and it soon split into three separate factions. Eighteen-year-old Owney Madden became the head of the largest one. His territory ranged from below 42nd Street and extended southward as far as the domain of his rival gang, the Hudson Dusters.

Madden was a bold and ruthless leader. Though his appearance was always neat and elegant, and though he possessed the gentle smile of a cherub, he was an exceptionally violent young man. By the time he took the reigns of the largest Gopher faction, he had already been a suspect in two murders. Skilled with all kinds of weapons, from guns and slingshots to blackjacks and brass knuckles, his favorite by far was a piece of lead pipe wrapped in a newspaper.

Not long after he took over a division of the Gophers, Madden was accused of murdering an Italian man for no other reason than to celebrate his newfound status as a gang leader. Knowing he couldn't afford to be imprisoned so soon after he'd achieved power, Madden ordered his men to silence anyone who might have witnessed the murder. Several crucial witnesses were subsequently convinced that it would be best for their own safety not to tell the police what they had seen. The police's sudden inability to locate the witnesses made it difficult for detectives to find enough evidence to take the case to trial. The charges were dropped and Madden was once again a free man — free to wreak more havoc.

A year later, Madden found himself at the center of another murder case after a young clerk named William Henshaw took an interest in a woman whom the gang leader had his eyes on. Madden wasn't about to let Henshaw get away with moving in on one of his girls. On February 4, 1912, two men gunned down the hapless clerk as he was about to board a streetcar. Henshaw was rushed to New York Hospital where, moments before taking his last breath, he identified Madden as his killer.

Perhaps because they had been unsuccessful at catching the gang leader in the past, the police didn't attempt to arrest Madden right away. This raised more than a few eyebrows, including those of Henshaw's father, who was shocked that it was taking authorities so long to catch his son's killer. Finally, more than a week after the murder occurred, the police made their move. After receiving a tip that Madden was on the roof of a building on West 33rd Street flying his pigeons, they rushed over to arrest him.

By the time they reached the address, Madden was no longer on the roof. The officers stuck around and kept an eye on the building, hoping he would reappear. Half an hour later, he was spotted running down the street. The police gave chase and caught him a few blocks later. But it was all for naught — charges against Madden were dropped when no witnesses to Henshaw's murder could be found.

Despite the fear he created wherever he went, Madden had plenty of enemies who were willing to stand up to him. Ambitious and domineering, he made no secret of his desire to rule over all the gangs, and this didn't sit well with other members of the underworld — especially those of the Hudson Dusters. Founded in the late 1890s by gangsters Kid Yorke, Circular Jack, and Goo Goo Knox, the Hudson Dusters were the Gophers' fiercest rivals, and they were keen to put an end to Madden's endless threats.

On November 6, 1912, Madden attended a dance hosted by the Dave Hyson Association at the Arbor Dance Hall. The Dave Hyson Association wasn't a legitimate organization. Rather, it was created as a way to beat the tax laws. It also allowed the hall's management to sell alcohol after hours, which was permitted only if a dance was being hosted by a legitimate social organization. To take advantage of this rule, waiters at the hall took turns creating an association under their name and hosting dances throughout the winter.

People at this particular winter dance were having a great time until Owney the Killer walked into the hall. Immediately uncomfortable, they watched as he strode to the middle of the dance floor and stood there with his arms folded. The music stopped and the partygoers held their breath, waiting. Then Madden waved his hand in a grand gesture. "Go on and have your fun!" he proclaimed. "I won't bump anybody off here tonight."

Madden walked upstairs and grabbed a seat in the balcony. It was a good spot — he could see what was going on in the hall and everyone could see him. He sat by himself for a while, drinking whiskey and watching the party unfold below. Women would shoot him coy glances, while other gangsters simply glared at him. Just after midnight, a pretty young woman joined him at his table. As she chatted away, Madden lost all interest in the goings-on around him. He was captivated by the girl sitting across from him — and she seemed taken with him, too. Eventually she went back downstairs, leaving him alone. Feeling relaxed and happy, he looked down at the party that was continuing below. Then he leisurely looked around the balcony where he was sitting. That's when he noticed the 11 men who had slipped upstairs and taken seats all around him while his attention was focused on the young woman. They were all members of the Hudson Dusters, and they surrounded him on three sides.

Knowing full well that they intended to kill him, Madden stood up slowly and faced his enemies. He wasn't about to go down quietly. "Come on, youse guys," he cried. "Youse wouldn't shoot nobody! Who did youse ever bump off?"

The tension broke when one of the men cursed. They opened fire, and Owney the Killer dropped to the floor and lost consciousness. He'd been hit half a dozen times. Leaving him for dead, the gunmen walked back downstairs and out the door of the Arbor Dance Hall.

The police arrived and brought the wounded leader of the Gophers to the hospital. Once Madden regained consciousness, a detective went to his bedside and demanded to know who had shot him. But Madden refused to reveal the identities of his attackers, insisting the matter wasn't anyone's business but his own. He would take care of things his own way. Less than a week after the shooting, 3 of the 11 gunmen were dead — the Gophers had avenged their leader.

As members of the Hudson Dusters were receiving their punishments, a small-time member of the Gophers was planning a move of his own. Madden had suffered serious injuries during the dance hall shooting. He needed time to convalesce. William "Little Patsy" Doyle saw his leader's period of recovery as an opportunity to gain control of the gang.

Ambition wasn't the only motive behind Doyle's plan. He also had a personal grudge against Madden. Doyle's girlfriend, Freda Horner, had recently left him for the leader of the Gophers. Still reeling from the rebuff, Doyle began to spread rumors that Madden had been permanently disabled by the attempt on his life. Doyle also began to work on his own image as a tough guy. After beating up a policeman, he was gratified and encouraged by the reactions of approval that he received from many of his fellow gang members. He then managed to gather together a small group of followers who were feeling a bit disgruntled with Madden's leadership, and prepared to stage his coup.

Madden, of course, found out what Doyle was doing. The head of the Gophers knew he had to act quickly or things might get out of hand. Not long after Madden was released from hospital, a group of loyal Gophers attacked Doyle with a lead pipe and nearly killed him.

Despite the attempt on his life, Doyle remained undeterred in his quest to unseat Madden and win back the heart of Freda Horner. In fact, he became even bolder in his efforts. He blackjacked some of Madden's favorite men, then slugged, stabbed, and shot a friend of Madden who had taunted him about Freda.

The leader of the Gophers wasn't about to let Doyle get away with these beatings. After all, his own credibility was at stake. Soon, rumors began circulating around Hell's Kitchen that Doyle was a snitch. Nobody, under any circumstance, wanted to be associated with a stool pigeon. One by one, Doyle's followers began to desert him and return to Madden's flock.

Killing Doyle's credibility wasn't enough for Madden. He met with two of his best marksmen — Art Biedler and Johnny McArdle — and assigned them the task of gunning down the traitor. Meanwhile, Freda Horner approached Margaret Everdeane, the girlfriend of a Gopher called Willie "the Sailor" Mott. Willie was a friend of Doyle. The two women were told to come up with a way to lure Doyle to a place where the gunmen could kill him. Once the plan was laid out, Margaret phoned Doyle and invited him to join her and Willie at a local saloon. She explained to Doyle that Freda felt bad about their breakup and wanted to see him.

On November 28, 1914, Doyle arrived at a West Side saloon just before midnight. As he entered, he didn't notice the three men waiting in the shadows across the street, or that two of them walked into the saloon less than five minutes after he'd entered.

Doyle walked past the bar and headed to the back room. As he approached Margaret and Willie's table, he noticed that Freda wasn't with them. When he asked where she was, Margaret told him to sit tight, Freda would be by shortly. A moment later, a bartender came over and told Doyle that someone was waiting for him at the bar. Following the bartender out of the back room, Doyle was promptly greeted by Biedler and McArdle's gunfire. The first bullet hit him in the lung, and he began to stagger. He was hit two more times before he fell to the floor. With great difficulty, Doyle managed to get to his feet, but when he tried to pull out his gun he was too weak to grasp it. Staggering along the bar, he made his way out of the saloon, but then died on the sidewalk. By then, Biedler and McArdle had fled the scene.

Madden was arrested soon after the hit, as were Margaret Everdeane, Freda Horner, Willie the Sailor, and the two gunmen. Johnny McArdle was sentenced to 13 years in prison and Art Biedler was given 18 years. Both had pleaded guilty to manslaughter. Madden, however, figured he could beat the rap yet again. He decided to plead not guilty when he was tried in 1915.

During his trial, Freda Horner and Margaret Everdeane took the stand as witnesses for the prosecution. They testified that Madden had ordered the hit on Little Patsy Doyle. Madden then took the stand in his own defense, but the prosecution destroyed his testimony. Frustrated, he let his hot temper get the better of him when he was caught in a lie. He jumped up from the witness stand to try to attack the prosecutor, but someone restrained him. Still proclaiming his innocence, he complained that he wasn't getting a fair trial and refused to continue testifying. Even prodding from his lawyer didn't help.

Madden was beginning to realize that he might not get off this time. Not sure of his next move, he requested to be taken out of the courtroom to a holding cell. He was then brought to the Tombs, where he was forced to stay until he was ready to complete his testimony. A few days later he returned to the stand, but his testimony did him little good. In short order, he was found guilty of manslaughter and sentenced to 10 to 20 years in Sing Sing. At the time of his sentencing, the 23-year-old leader of the Gophers was believed to have committed five murders.

Madden was a model prisoner, spending much of his time tending to a flock of pigeons that he was allowed to keep in jail. He was granted early parole and released on January 22, 1923. He was quick to discover, however, that the underworld had changed during his imprisonment. The Gophers had disappeared, and the days of rival gangs duking it out on city streets and in local watering holes were over. The rough and ready street gangs had been replaced by business-savvy gangsters who were making money hand over fist in the illicit liquor trade that flourished during Prohibition.

Realizing the vast opportunities to be had in the liquor trade, Madden returned to the West Side and got involved in bootlegging. He founded Harlem's infamous Cotton Club, which featured first-rate performers such as Duke Ellington and Cab Calloway. He later moved to the tourist resort of Hot Springs, Arkansas, where he took a piece of the profits at local casinos. Owney the Killer Madden died of natural causes in 1965. He remained influential and respected by gangsters until the end, hosting underworld figures like Al Capone and Charles "Lucky" Luciano whenever such men needed a place to lie low.

Chapter 7
Arnold Rothstein: The Original Don

It was Saturday, May 15, 1920, and gangster Arnold Rothstein was cheekily driving his flashy blue Cadillac down Fifth Avenue at the tail end of the annual police parade. With him was his friend Nicky Arnstein, who was facing charges of engineering bond thefts on Wall Street totaling $5 million. Arnstein's wife, actress Fanny Brice, and attorney William J. Fallon were also in the car. The foursome was on their way to the Criminal Courts Building to arrange for Arnstein's bail.

Upon reaching their destination, Rothstein parked the car in front of a saloon across the street. As he and Arnstein headed for the Criminal Courts Building, the other two went into the saloon to wait for their companions. Brice and Fallon were inside enjoying their drinks when they looked out the saloon window and realized someone had stolen Rothstein's Cadillac. They were both stunned at the audacity of the thieves. Immediately, phone calls were made to spread the word that the stolen vehicle belonged to Arnold Rothstein. Surely when the thieves realized who actually owned the car they would think twice about keeping it.

Within half an hour, four gangsters came back to the scene of the crime and returned the car. One of them was Monk Eastman, the former head of the Eastman Gang. He apologized profusely to Rothstein's lawyer. The thieves hadn't known the car belonged to Rothstein, he explained. If they had known, they never would have taken it in the first place.

Gangsters throughout New York City and the rest of the U.S. both feared and respected Arnold Rothstein. He wasn't someone you wanted to mess with. Not only did Rothstein have connections with high-ranking politicians and prominent criminals, he bankrolled the illegal activities of many of New York's gangs. Many have claimed that he was the most powerful criminal of his era — and the mastermind behind modern organized crime.

Arnold "the Brain" Rothstein was born in a brownstone on East 47th Street in Manhattan in 1882, the second of six children in a middle-class Orthodox Jewish family. Growing up, he didn't really like school, but always enjoyed math. "He loved to play with numbers," his brother Edgar later recalled. This love would serve him well when he went into the gambling and loan sharking business later on.

Rothstein made money by lending it to other gamblers at phenomenally high interest rates. He also masterminded bond robberies and investment frauds that saw innocent investors bilked of millions of dollars. Over the years, he became the man to see about financing illegal business ventures.

Early in his career, Rothstein cultivated a friendship with powerful East Side politician Timothy "Big Tim" Sullivan, as well as with other political figures. These relationships made Rothstein all the more influential, allowing him to conduct his illegal activities virtually unimpeded. He used his growing bankroll to buy off his political friends and control policing.

By 1919, Rothstein had become extremely powerful in New York City's underworld. Not only did he have the money to finance illegal activities, and the necessary political connections to proceed with these activities, he also had the organizational skills and business acumen to pull it all off. And prime opportunities to make really big money were just around the corner.

On October 28, 1919, the National Prohibition Enforcement Act (also known as the Volstead Act) was passed. This act, which banned the manufacture, sale, or transportation of intoxicating liquors within national borders, went into effect on January 16, 1920, and it would forever change the way that gangs and gangsters operated in the United States — thanks in large part to Arnold Rothstein.

In the fall of 1919, Rothstein was approached by a face from the past. Irving Wexler, a.k.a Waxey Gordon, came to him with a business proposition. Gordon had worked with Rothstein as a labor enforcer in the garment district years earlier and had since served time in prison. A former pickpocket and unrepentant thug, Gordon was certain that he was destined for big things. With Prohibition on the horizon, he and fellow gangster Big Max Greenberg wanted to set up a large rum-running business in Detroit. The plan was to buy liquor in Canada and sell it throughout the United States, but they needed $175,000 to get started. The only person they knew who had that kind of money was Rothstein. Gordon and Greenberg were aware that Rothstein charged exorbitant interest rates, but there was simply no one else who could finance their new business venture. Their operation would also require organization, people, and protection — the likes of which had probably never before been seen in the underworld.

Waxey Gordon contacted Rothstein, who agreed to hear what the two men had to say. He met them on a bench in Central Park and listened carefully to their proposal. When their pitch was done, he arranged to meet them in his office the following day. Greenberg and Gordon's timing was fortuitous. The Brain already had it in his head that hefty profits were to be made in rum-running. He knew Prohibition wouldn't quench Americans' thirst for good whiskey.

The next day, Rothstein made the two gangsters a counterproposal. Rather than buying whiskey from Canadian middlemen who would only eat away at Rothstein's profits, they would run their operation out of New York. The best Scotch whiskey would be bought directly from distillers in Britain and shipped to the United States to be sold. Rothstein didn't want to sell cheap liquor. He wanted to build a sound business based on supplying the best whiskey to the people who could afford to buy it. He agreed to bankroll the operation, but informed Gordon and Greenberg that he would also be involved in importing and distributing the Scotch, and that he would head up the illegal smuggling operation. Moreover, he would arrange to pay officials to look the other way and provide bail and lawyers if things went wrong. The men agreed to his offer, for Rothstein was a difficult man to refuse. This deal marked the beginning of modern organized crime in the United States.

Now that the three men had agreed to team up, they needed to find someone who could buy the liquor in Europe and ship it to the United States. Rothstein hired Henry Mather, a native of the Lower East Side who was lying low in England to avoid charges of running an illegal investment operation. Mather bought 20,000 cases of Scotch from distillers and hired a ship to get them across the Atlantic. A flotilla of smaller speedboats was waiting for the ship just outside the American three-mile territorial limit, off Long Island's east coast.

The illegal cargo was loaded onto the speedboats and ferried under the cover of darkness to a convoy of trucks waiting onshore. Rothstein had bribed the Coast Guard, state troopers, and police in Suffolk and Nassau Counties to turn a blind eye to the operation, so the smugglers didn't have to worry about interference. He also hired gangsters Jack "Legs" Diamond and his brother Eddie to guard the convoy as the contraband hooch was loaded up and brought to warehouses in the city.

Waxey Gordon oversaw the operation, which made 10 successful crossings. Then Rothstein got word that a new Coast Guard commander was being stationed at Long Island's Montauk Point headquarters. The new boss had been ordered to put a stop to the smuggling and seize Rothstein's shipments. With preparations for the 11th shipment already underway, Rothstein began to worry. After some hasty orchestrating, he arranged to have the shipment diverted to Cuba, but realized shortly after that he just couldn't control the business. Though he continued to help finance operations, he ended his partnership with Gordon and Greenberg and left the day-to-day rum-running — including operating a warehouse in the city and another one on Long Island — to Gordon. Rothstein was now making considerable profits from rum-running, but without the risk.

Meanwhile, late in 1921, the Diamond brothers decided it was pointless to invest in the illicit liquor trade. The time commitment and large sums of money involved in buying liquor, smuggling it into the United States, and paying law enforcement officials to look the other way just didn't seem to be worth the end result. They had a better idea. Why not simply hijack someone else's cargo once it reached American soil? It wasn't like the smugglers would be in a hurry to complain to authorities that their liquor had been stolen.

With Prohibition well underway and lots of people trying to cash in, this approach would allow the Diamonds to make money with very little overhead. All they needed were a few trucks to haul away their loot, some warehouses to stash the goods, and a network to distribute and sell the liquor. With Rothstein only too happy to supply the cash and back the distribution network, they were all set. They hired other up-and-coming gangsters to help them, including Lucky Luciano and Dutch Schultz.

Whenever the Diamond brothers got arrested, Rothstein hired lawyers to represent them in court and provided the money to bail them out. But brushes with the law weren't their only worry. Some of the liquor smugglers were none too happy about having their cargo hijacked. A carload of gunmen caught up with Legs Diamond in the fall of 1924. They fired at him on 110th Street and 5th Avenue, peppering the right side of his head with birdshot. Despite being wounded, Diamond managed to drive himself to Mount Sinai Hospital. He was treated and released, and he soon recovered from his wounds. Rothstein and the Diamond brothers eventually parted ways. Without the Brain's protection, the Diamonds' gang began to fade.

Having abandoned the role of active rum-runner, Rothstein turned his attention to new ventures. The 1914

Harrison Narcotics Act had been legislated to put a stop to the domestic drug trade, but it had left more than half a million opiate addicts without a place to get their fix. Most of them were white, middle-aged, middle-class women. These women needed access to drugs and fed a growing demand for illegal narcotics. Gangsters Lucky Luciano and Waxey Gordon saw that there was business potential in supplying drugs to addicts and told Rothstein about it.

Never one to miss out on a chance to make money, the Brain set his sights on drug trafficking. He wasn't terribly interested in having men standing out on street corners pushing drugs. It was more the wholesaling end of the business that grabbed his attention. Rothstein wanted to organize the drug trade on an international level, controlling the supply and demand in the United States. He contacted Harry Mather, his rum-running agent, and had him comb the European continent in search of reliable drug suppliers. However, China soon became his primary source for supplies. Rothstein sent Sidney Stajer, Jacob "Yasha" Katzenberg, and veteran drug dealer George Uffner to Asia to set up the network.

Once he had made contact with suppliers overseas, Rothstein needed a way to bring the goods into the United States. He purchased a well-established New York importing house called Vantine's, which dealt primarily in antiques. The shipments coming to Vantine's from China were barely inspected by customs officials, making them ideal for smuggling in drugs. Rothstein sought out contracts for home furnishings, which would provide an opportunity to stash drugs in a shipment. He also bought more antique shops and galleries to serve as fronts for his drug business.

A side effect of Rothstein's newest venture was that it improved his bail bonding business — men who were arrested on drug offenses would turn to him for money. Rothstein had them coming and going.

It was not long, however, before federal narcotics agents got word that illegal drugs were being imported into the United States. In July 1926, they raided the loft of a toy company on Walker Street. There they found five crates filled with narcotics. The crates, labeled "bowling balls and pins," had been shipped from Germany to New York aboard the White Star liner *Arabia*. Rothstein associates Charles Webber and William Vachuda were arrested, and Rothstein promptly posted their bail. It was alleged that Webber and Vachuda had imported more than two tons of illegal narcotics — the bulk of the American drug trade — between February and August 1926. Webber was sentenced to 14 years in prison and Vachuda received 8 years. Neither breathed a word of their connection to Rothstein.

Despite the raid, life was good for Rothstein. He had been mentoring up-and-coming gangsters like Frank Costello, Lucky Luciano, and Meyer Lansky — men who would later play key roles in the underworld. Rothstein taught these men how to organize an illegal operation at the lowest cost and do away with the competition. And he also helped Luciano out financially, lending him $21,000 in 1928.

Rothstein was a very busy man, but he still found time to gamble. In September 1928, he participated in a craps and poker session hosted by bookmaker and gambler George "Hump" McManus. The other participants in the marathon session were Alvin C. "Titanic" Thompson, Meyer Boston and his brother Sam, "Red Martin" Bowe, and Nathan "Nigger Nate" Raymond. The men began betting on Saturday night. By the time their epic session ended two days later, on the morning of Monday, September 10, Rothstein was the big loser — he had accrued $322,000 in gambling debts.

Rothstein, who loved to collect money but hated to pay, suggested that the game had been rigged. This accusation was meant as more than just an insult to his fellow gamblers. By insinuating that he'd been bilked, Rothstein was trying to get out of paying his hefty debt. Weeks went by, and still Rothstein refused to pay. The other players grew increasingly impatient and began calling him to demand their money.

On Sunday, November 4, 1928, Rothstein sat in his office and took out a $50,000 life insurance policy on himself. Then he went to Lindy's restaurant on Seventh Avenue to take care of some business. Lindy's was a popular meeting place for all sorts of New Yorkers, including actors, songwriters, gamblers, and journalists. Rothstein often conducted business there, meeting with his associates at the same booth every time. That night, Rothstein arrived at Lindy's at around 9 p.m. When the phone rang at 10:15, Rothstein spoke quietly to the person on the other end for about a minute, then he hung up, put on his hat and coat, and headed to the Park Central Hotel.

Just before 11 p.m., Vince Kelly, the service elevator operator at the Park Central, saw a man walking slowly down the stairs near the hotel's employees' entrance. The man was holding his side, and Kelly couldn't figure out if he was ill or drunk. Kelly asked the stranger if he was sick. "I've been shot," he replied, and then asked for a taxi.

At that moment, the hotel's night watchman and its house detective arrived on the scene. Both immediately recognized the wounded man as Arnold Rothstein. One of them ran outside and came back with Ninth Precinct patrolman William M. Davis. When Davis asked Rothstein who had shot him, Rothstein refused to reply. He just wanted to go home.

More than an hour after he'd been shot, he was loaded into an ambulance and taken to the Polyclinic Hospital. The bullet was removed from Rothstein's abdomen, but the damage was already done — the slug had severed an artery, causing massive internal bleeding. Rothstein lingered in a semi-comatose state for about 36 hours. He died on the morning of November 6, 1928, at the age of 46. He was buried the next day at Union Field Cemetery in Queens. No one was ever convicted of his murder.

After Rothstein's death, one of his employees took it upon himself to go through the Brain's personal files and remove some of the more damaging documents. The papers that were left behind, however, revealed a great deal of shocking information, including Rothstein's ties to Tammany Hall politicians, judges, and members of the underworld. Towards the end of November, New York district attorney Joab Banton announced publicly that his office would study Rothstein's files. However, upon learning that Tammany Hall politician Tom Foley was incriminated in the files, Banton did an about-face and announced that they were of no interest to his office. Foley, it turned out, had been instrumental in helping Banton land his job.

If Banton couldn't use any of the information in Rothstein's files, the United States district attorney's office certainly could. After poring over the papers, federal authorities were able to apprehend a number of the Brain's contacts. On December 7, 1928, Rothstein associate Joseph Unger checked two large steamer trunks and boarded a train for Chicago. Waiting agents, working on the information contained in Rothstein's files, opened up the trunks and found $2 million worth of heroin, opium, and cocaine. Unger was arrested at 11 p.m. as the train was nearing Buffalo.

Meanwhile, other agents raided a room at the Hotel North Sheridan in Chicago and confiscated $500,000 in drugs. Eleven days later, federal agents seized a large shipment of drugs that had arrived on a Jersey City pier in boxes labeled "scrubbing brushes."

In the end, Rothstein's papers helped federal agents intercept illegal shipments valued at $7 million and uncover an intricate smuggling network with a trail leading to a number of major U.S. cities (including Boston, Philadelphia, Detroit, Chicago, and San Francisco) and foreign countries. Joseph Unger was brought back to New York, where the U.S. district attorney hoped to interrogate him and learn more about the extent of the drug ring. Unger pleaded guilty to possessing and transporting opium on December 21, 1928, but refused to reveal anything about Rothstein's narcotics business.

By this time, prompted by Rothstein's teachings, a number of gang leaders in New York and on the East Coast had begun working together. Lucky Luciano headed a seven-member alliance, which also included Frank Costello, Bugsy Siegel, Meyer Lansky, and Waxey Gordon. The Big Seven, as it was known, had developed alliances with 22 gangs along the East Coast of the United States.

Arnold Rothstein, the original don, left an indelible mark on New York's underworld. He brought the underworld into the modern era, moving criminal activity away from haphazard street crimes to more organized affairs that used administrative skills to build a criminal empire. The men he tutored would mark his legacy by adopting and expanding his business approach. The days of neighborhood gangs battling it out on the streets of New York for a piece of turf had evolved. Thanks to Rothstein, crime had become a business enterprise.

Further Reading

Asbury, Herbert. *The Gangs of New York*. New York: Thunder's Mouth Press, 1927.

Downey, Patrick. *Gangster City*. Fort Lee, New Jersey: Barricade Books Inc., 2004.

Katcher, Leo. *The Big Bankroll: The Life and Times of Arnold Rothstein*. New York: Harper and Brothers, 1959.

Kenny, Dennis J., and James O. Finckenauer. *Organized Crime in America*. Belmont, California: Wadsworth Publishing Company, 1995.

McIllwain, Jeffrey Scott. *Organizing Crime in Chinatown: Race and Racketeering in New York City, 1890–1910*. Jefferson, North Carolina: McFarland & Company, Inc., 2004.

Peterson, Virgil W. *The Mob: 200 Years of Organized Crime in New York*. Ottawa, Illinois: Green Hill Publishers, Inc., 1983.

Pietrusza, David. *Rothstein*. New York: Carroll & Graf Publishers, 2003.

Sante, Luc. *Low Life*. New York: Farrar, Straus & Giroux, 2003.

Acknowledgments

My thanks to all of the researchers, authors, and journalists who have tackled — and continue to tackle — the subject of gangs and organized crime in New York and elsewhere around the world. Your work tells us so much about how far we have come — and how much further we have to go. As one Montreal crime reporter knows all too well, organized crime is not to be taken lightly. He very nearly paid with his life for his dedication to trying to tell the truth about biker gangs.

I appreciate the confidence that my editor at Altitude, Jill Foran, associate publisher Kara Turner, and publisher Stephen Hutchings have shown in me. They thought that my criminology background would be a terrible thing to waste — and I agree. Thank you for giving me the opportunity to bring together my field of study and my need to write.

Thank you to my family for encouraging me to be whatever I want to be, and for sharing in the joys of getting there. My friend Barbara Bunce Desmeules deserves special mention for making me laugh harder than anyone else as I got closer to my deadline for finishing the book. Humor is a great antidote to stress.

Author's Note

The activities of gangs and organized crime have been glamorized through books, films, and television. I have made every effort to be as accurate as possible, and to separate fact from fiction.

About the Author

Hélèna Katz is an award-winning Montreal journalist whose work has appeared in magazines and newspapers in Canada and the United States. She earned a Bachelor of Arts degree in psychology from McGill University and is currently a Masters candidate in criminology at the Université de Montréal. She is the author of *The Mad Trapper: The Incredible Tale of a Famous Canadian Manhunt.*

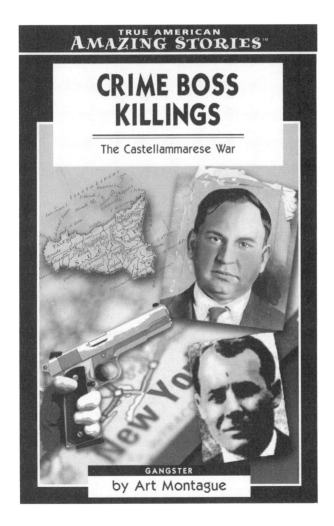

ISBN 1-55265-101-0